OXYGEN

To the Welsh poets of tomorrow.
I feirdd dyfodol Cymru.

OXYGEN

**beirdd newydd o gymru
new poets from wales**

**english editor: amy wack
golygydd gymraeg: grahame davies**

seren

seren
is the book imprint of
Poetry Wales Press Ltd
Wyndham Street, Bridgend, Wales

Editorial, selection & Introductions © Amy Wack
and Grahame Davies, 2000

The poems © the respective poets

ISBN 1-85411-284-8

A CIP record for this title is available from
the British Library

*The publisher works with the financial assistance of the
Arts Council of Wales*

Cover Image: Juliane Gregor

Printed in Palatino by
WBC Book Manufacturers, Bridgend

CONTENTS/CYNNWYS

Kate Bingham

Owen Sheers

Karen Goodwin

Emyr Lewis

Iwan Llwyd

Introduction

Fresh air! A culture thrives or dies on the strength of its young writers. This anthology simply aims to represent the best poetry by a new generation that has appeared in Wales over the past decade or so. The authors featured here are under 45 years of age, all have or are about to, publish individual collections or pamphlets. Several do not originate from Wales, but have lived or worked here for a considerable time. Their voices, temperaments, viewpoints, styles, means and methods are refreshingly varied. The English language poets here seem less concerned than previous generations with questions of identity. Their confidence is manifest in poems that view Wales with an ironic affection, if not a humour that approaches parody. They are the children of the information age. Their tastes are sophisticated and rarely plain. One may note a very recent shift away from the poem as word-game or technical pirouette, towards a less oblique emotionalism; there are a surprising number of love poems here. Also of note is the predominance of · women writers, particularly in the youngest third of the contributors. This reflects international trends. For a country with a population of approximately three million, as compared to about 15 million in the greater London area, and five million in Scotland, Wales does reasonably well in the production of poets. We do have some way to go in fostering a cultural climate as favourable to them as those in Dublin or Edinburgh.

These young writers do share with an earlier generation of fine poets like Sheenagh Pugh, Robert Minhinnick, Hilary Llewellyn-Williams, Paul Groves, Duncan Bush, Christopher Meredith, John Davies, Peter Finch and Tony Curtis, a shocking under-representation in British anthologies from ostensibly major publishers, a deficit we hope this book helps address. We also hope to foster some cross pollination of interests between the younger Welsh language poets, whose works are rarely available in translation, and their counterparts who write in that upstart tongue, English. My special thanks to the authors featured, particularly to Kate Bingham, whose poem provided us with our title. Thanks are also due to the Seren staff, Cary Archard, Mick Felton, Simon Hicks and Lisa Jones, and to Welsh Editor Grahame Davies for all of their hard work and invaluable advice.

Amy Wack

Cyflwyniad

In putting together the Welsh language section of this collection, I have tried to represent the major figures, styles and themes of the younger generation of Welsh poets so as to introduce them to those unfamiliar with the field. This is not an exact science, and the exigencies of translation make the anthologist's task all the more difficult, so the selection is conditioned not merely by factors such as theme, quality, and representativeness, but also by the question of how well the poems will translate.

As is sometimes said, poetry is that which is lost in translation, and this is particularly true of the Welsh strict metres, or *cynghanedd*, the intricate form of internal rhyme and alliteration which has existed in Welsh poetry since at least the sixth century, and which has enjoyed a marked revival among the very generation of poets included here. Around a quarter of the poems in this collection were originally in *cynghanedd*. That is probably an unrepresentatively small proportion of the total available material, but the anthology had to aim at presenting successful translations, not dutiful renditions of poems which remain essentially untranslatable. This accounts for the omission of some notable names from the generation of the *cynghanedd* revival: for instance, Dafydd John Pritchard, Tudur Dylan Jones, Gwenallt Llwyd Ifan and Dafydd Evan Morris were all considered at length for inclusion, but the rigours of their original metres proved too much for the translation process. The inclusion of the work of Ceri Wyn Jones, Huw M. Edwards, Meirion MacIntyre Huws and Nici Beech may therefore be taken as representative of this school. Difficulty of translation is also the reason why some other poets who operate extensively in *cynghanedd*, such as Twm Morys and Emyr Lewis, are represented here mainly by work in other metres.

13

As for themes, two issues specific to the Welsh-language context need to be highlighted. Firstly, there is a wealth of humorous and public poetry in Welsh, and an attempt has been made to represent it here with poems such as Meirion MacIntyre Huws' "Côt", Twm Morys' "Sefyll 'Rown" and Ifor ap Glyn's "Tri Darlleniad Trychinebus Ynys Prydain". Secondly, many of the poems here address questions of politics, identity and culture which are crucial to the condition of belonging to a minority linguistic community, in this case, a community of some 500,000 Welsh-speakers, one-fifth of the Welsh population. By and large, the poems deal with such issues with a resilience and humour characteristic of the new-found confidence exemplified by the *cynghanedd* revival itself. As a whole, I believe this collection shows Welsh-language poets engaging, via both traditional and newer forms, not only with the concerns of their particular culture, but with the broader conditions of the Western society we all share and with questions common to people of all cultures, and I believe that this displays the continuing vigour and promise of the poetry of the older of the two main languages of Wales.

I would like to thank the poets for their ready co-operation, and, in many cases, for their translations of their own poems. I am very grateful also to the translators, Elin ap Hywel and Richard Poole, for their sensitive work. Finally, special thanks are due to my fellow editor, Amy Wack, not only for her perceptive editing of the contributions but also for the hard work of co-ordinating the production of the whole volume.

Grahame Davies

OLIVER REYNOLDS

Reading

Within the dark night, a house.
Within that, a room with one corner lit.
Within that, my head and a book.

And then this, the strangest recession:
I am there, but not there.
I am reading.

"It takes you out of yourself."
Easy as taking a hand out of a pocket.
But hands don't float off.

Dark clamours at the window.
Moths batter the bulb.
I read on.

My body dwindles.
Thinned by text, it becomes Euclidean:
It has position but no magnitude.

An hour later, it returns;
Slowly, as if dropping by parachute.
I yawn and head for the toilet.

In bed, I pull up the blankets.
Night's tribunes call the room to order.
The moths stutter across the wall.

I have read too much.
Asleep, I read on.
Words and images dribble on to the pillow.

The left arm of Michelangelo's David
Was broken into pieces by a bench
Hurled from the Palazzo Vecchio.

Restored, the arm now burns.
The white marble has a dark skin of smoke.
The hand waves through the flames.

The Player Queen's Wife

(for Tone)

Our stage was Europe,
dragging from country to country
in a cart sold off by a rain-broken farmer
and trusting to the company's seven languages
(Garbo, a Gypsy and our Fool, had four of them).

A life spent trailing a cart
or, pregnant again, bouncing inside it
on a mattress of dusty curtains;
a life of haggling with innkeepers;
of naming the yearly children
after old Gods and dead actors;
of days stalled by a river
waiting for it to go down,
brown water thrashing like an animal's back.

And then, having come through mountains
or reached the steepled horizon across the plain
or that castle up on its crags
where the creeping Jesus in black
told us our own job — with actions —
once we'd arrived and unpacked,
made our bargain and beaten our drum,
I'd watch a stubbly queen
make me presents of myself:

daydreaming, she'd stop half-way
through pulling up a stocking
(as I've done, thinking of home)
or, laughing, splay her fringe (the best wig)
with a gesture I've had since a girl
or finally, at the bows and curtsies,
she'd grin and lift her skirts
to show again the stockings
I thought I'd lost two towns ago.

The Gap

It's H and I've O.D.'d —
   Intravenous, straight to the heart —
And here I am stumbling toward an ode,
   A paean in reverse, a hymn to hurt,
Here I am, weepy, wondering, writing
   Out of love, out of loss,
      Out of my one-track mind, its rails empty
And aimed at a future as unwitting
   As you are, now you're all but dead to me,
      Now you're with someone else.

That douce rainbow of olive and tan, white and black
   Is the clothes you buy at The Gap
I see now, minus the labels at waist and neck
   You would remove by a surgical rip
With that de-stitching tool straight out of Bosch,
   Fanged steel ensuring skin was kissed
      By nothing but Cotton, 100%.
My wallet saved one label (a cheque never cashed)
   Till the day it gets binned: when I'm absent-
      Minded with loss, or brave, or rash.

Your white jeans had a workman's loop, handy for
                                    a hammer,
   Which, climbing into a cab ("Chinatown..."),
Snagged, and the seam gave, and gave me more:
   A private road to Paradise which, serpentine,
I took, exploring this gap, this fissure
   For my fingers, for the aficionado
      I am of you: your skin, your yawn, your laugh,
Your fugues of boredom, your sharpening into desire —
   While I could be wondering whether we'd make love,
      You'd want to fuck without further ado.

Soup for starters, four smoky bowls of hot-and-sour —
   Kim's choice — and this out-of-sync match, this pact
Of opposites, recalls the face I've seen Kim wear

Listening to poetry, the face I call Baffled Respect.
So we ate and talked. And it was clear that Angela,
  Kim's wife, was not your type (and you weren't hers).
    China spoons chinked on china bowls.
You didn't like what she did to him: "She defers."
  I like, and dislike, how your heart rebels
    At conciliation: how it's spiky, cold, angular.

But I fret whether not having a heart to give
  Means not having a heart, Helen, at all.
(Is this hurt, putting on airs? Or love?
  Or my usual knack for being fatal?)
I fret about what's not there — my face has the gape
  Of the opening door pushed at too late
    As we collect all that is lost and last
And walk into that space where the ribs hug a gap
  The size of a fist, and inside that fist
    Random stars wait, infinite and unlit.

Greek

A headland. Heat. A single tree
drawn by the wind like a catapult
never to be released.

Then the sea's furnace-shimmer
heaves up this: the messenger
with his ingots of speech.

Throughout the rigmarole
of monsters and maidens
the commander unrolls maps.

The messenger is imperturbable
as an arrow. He is his mouth.
His wrecked body weighs no more

than an echo. Words
engorge his tongue
till he stops. Dead. Dumb.

The Almost

I had a gift which I didn't give you —
Rembrandt's Elephant extending his flirty trunk
like a trombonist, a glad-hander or a drunk
with a brolly. Who we are is what we do.
This benign clown hauling a favoured prop
from the scuffed grey suitcase of himself
is all elephant; this life left on the shelf
is me; and you... You are where the metaphors stop.
You are you. My gift went ungiven on a day
of waste, of feeling all but unwanted
from the moment I woke and heard you say
"I forgot you were here." So solidly planted
at the centre of ourselves, is it the self we betray
or each other — gifts not given, lives not granted?

Lugubrious troopers, tail-to-trunk, trunk-to-tail,
on pillared legs, like bridges walking,
the pachyderms of memory sail
into view, unbudgeably huge, baulking
at nothing. That morning, I remember,
I checked my watch — your gift to me — and saw
it had stopped. Time whitened into permanent December.
Half-asleep when you left, I heard you lock the door.
Rogue omens clashed their tusks. What did they mean?
That farewell forgetting — did you want me
not there at all, or there for good? Come clean —
what am I to you? I slept. A key dreamily
resolved each lock and clock, each clenched machine
of the self. It was cool in your palm. Ivory.

Your palm. Your hand. My face nuzzles your hand
and your fingers tighten: my mouth quenched by
                                                your palm
or your fingers drinking my face? Wellings-up. Balm.
The solitary cloud above arid land
with its promise, its blessing of water.
You wear your mother's wedding-ring with a plain band
annulling it. Your palm is boundless, a dream land

19

where the weather is knowledge: your daughter
has her mother's hands. She lifts them above her head,
blameless, blessing and blessed. She is a babe in arms —
in your perfect arms; she is sixteen; she is dead.
Farewell was a final touching of palms,
then our one child was christened by a thief.
He took our girl and he christened her: Grief.

Grief-greys lost in white-out: elephants move
across tundra into the true north of the mind.
Blizzards of self. White lies as love
winters out; the thinned air it leaves behind.
The animals approach a secret death,
their pensive tracks obscured by pensive snow.
Farewell is the cold blossoming of breath
in this graveyard where the forgotten go,
the hurt, the harmed, the outcast from the herd.
The two of us turn in our sleep. A ghost
turns with us, the sleepless ghost of a third.
The might-have-been. The all-but. The almost.
Our bedside candle is the wavering doubt
lovemaking left us too tired to blow out.

A cigarette on the shores of the Med —
you're weighing up the sea, all but undressed,
paddling, smoking and, mostly, unimpressed.
An Amazon's arms and a big cat's head —
flat-of-the-sword muscle and the slow-lidded blink
of puma or panther. You take my breath away
and hold it, breathing, in your mouth: each day
a fresh kill. I never know what you think.
We're old flames stalking each other — big game
purring repletion, sucking out marrow.
What seems a cry could be a cried-out name.
You dive. Sea-glints waver like a shuffled Tarot
till you surface, doing the butterfly: the same
quick-strung armspan loosing arrow after arrow.

Four ton of whimsy. Though the eye in its crow's nest
of wrinkles is friendly, the trunk's salutation
unsettles the onlookers: three ghosts dressed
in feints of chalk. Their robes might be Asian;
their faces are faceless; and there I am
among them, anonymous to myself,
self-doubting, an unfilled outline, a clam —
true by indirection, faithful by stealth.
Beware of unwise men bearing gifts (guilt,
indifference and hurt): beware of me.
We sift the sky for lost kingdoms. A silt
of stars hides the one star at apogee,
this mirage of a life like water spilled
in the star-grains of Sinai or Gobi.

Rilke: Evening

Like old retainers, trees
hold out day's evening dress
while the fading view
wavers between heaven and earth

and leaves you not quite part of either,
neither the quiet of the dark house
nor the grave certainty of light
of the rising star

that leaves you, voluble and dumb,
in the deserts and gardens of your life
alternating border with vista
and the stone in you with the star.

CATHERINE FISHER

In a Chained Library

Here they are, chained as if dangerous,
creatures from a bestiary left open,
foxed and gilded, a tangle of tails,
mouths, claws, spilling from the shelves.

Silent as unicorns their sweet unspoken music.
Finger them, the dry crackle of their skins.
Dragons burn in margins, sea-cats uncoil;
monsters, eating letters, being letters,

as if word and flesh and beast were one
and might burst out, huge and scaly,
slithering from the nave into the crowded streets,
scorching the night with a Babel of lost songs.

I. 13th April 1769. Matavai, Oteheite

(from *The Unexplored Ocean*: inspired by the Journals
of James Hartshill, an officer serving on His Majesty's
Ships *Endeavour* and *Resolution*, 1768-1779)

Charlotte, I wish you could see these people!
Their ocean is blue, so blue, deeper than
the gown you wore at Rookham;
the splash and lift of it nudges the ship;
their hills an uprush of trees
mirrored in the calm lagoon where we lilt at anchor.

They came out in canoes, waving and shouting;
some of them swam, and Gore who knows them,
swung in the rigging, laughing; the men silent
for once, lining the rails in amazement.
My sweet, the women are slim and brown,
the warriors feathered with the wings of scarlet birds.

22

They're all over the ship; as I write they watch,
laughing at my coat and the buckles on my shoes,
stealing, seducing, sudden and dangerous as children.
I find myself asking if this is Eden,
where sin is only the breaking of strange taboos.
The thought disturbs me, here without you.

I asked Forster if Hell was knowledge or none.
He laughed, said he had not voyaged so far,
nor hoped to. And they have given the captain
a feather cloak, and he bows so gravely.
Tomorrow he says, we unship the equipment
and six marines to guard it night and day.

It's dark now: the paper glimmers like pearl.
Already, love, the island has hold of me.
Its warm scents drift, sweet and strange,
into all the timbers of the ship; a creeping disorder,
a swaying dance. It upsets me, keeps me awake.
And I cannot laugh at myself as I would like.

Cimabue's Crucifix

(damaged in the Florence floods, 1966)

The water wears his hands; furrows his face.
It seeps into the wood of him, cracks and seams
swelling, splitting the still boards.
Slowly it infiltrates his beauty, lifting
gold leaf with infinite patience, flake
by flake; soaking the pigments away.

Water opens him. He's saturated,
running into long unwinding colours,
downward bruises, red and ochre;
shoulders sagging under the sopping weight.
Faces of saints, all the long night,
chin on palms, fragment in sympathy.

They're together now, loosened, dissolved;
so mingled that they'll never be apart.
The long work's over, he's come down, become
gold scum, splinters, one painted eye
floating in the wave-slap of the nave.
Outside, the world's a dripping day,

the city soaked and grey, and he slips
into the drains of it, the streets and alleyways,
the stinking houses; out of the hoses
slinking through hopeless hands. On
the walls of drowned piazzas a gold smear
marks the heights to which he's risen.

Undertakers

The baker's doorway steams like Acheron.
They eat hot rolls and pasties, shiny grease
soaking the paper so their fingers tear it;
the thin one smokes, flicking off ash.
Their coats are raven, crypt-black, but they laugh,
swap jokes, wave at a passing van.
Later they crowd the car
running its engines so the windows trickle;
one gazes at the bookie's, wistfully.

They've done their part; performed
the silent secrets no-one asks about.
Now through fiery glass the final hymn
brings them out to stamp, rub hands,
uncrease coats and faces.
They line the porch, pull on gloves,
leave the singing to others;
their tribute no emotion and firm hands,
sharing unsteadily on shoulders
the box of dark that always weighs too much,
and comes too soon.

Fimbulwinter

Sweating between towns on country roads
you learn your place. The hedge,
the slipstream, the exhaust.
You shouldn't be walking here, have no right;
read in exasperated glances and close shaves
your offence, though all the pilgrims, peddlers,
vagabonds in you rise up and spit.
Sidling to a bend you hold your breath
and the rucksack tight. Lorries roar
like dragons. Hawthorn shrivels,
each leaf a frenzy of dust.

These are the only roads
to where you need to go, a *via dolorosa*
between hedgerows where no buses run
and no-one stops, and where no voices are.
A gate's relief. You trespass in the grass,
see how we've shrunk our comings and our goings
to grey intent, shortest way
between two points, the land
by-passed, all stories left untold.

Maybe it's come closer than we think,
that time of no compassion for each other;
the wind-age, wolf-age, long destruction
that all cultures fear. Maybe the
monsters have been loosed and no-one noticed.
On Hell's road all men tremble; on this
field's edge the littered hedgerow holds
its stubborn line. There's no protection;
no-one's spoken since you left the town.
The only words are huge, stretch into distance.
Stop, they say. Give way. Give way.

Vampire Ballet

The dancer's squirming back. He's on his knees.
Music is a heartbeat, fascination.
The whole theatre's tense. No-one breathes.

It's that other man our eyes are on,
the dark one. Relentless he stalks
us all across the stage. As the music's torn

to pieces see him slither into smoke.
We feed off him, just as he feeds off us;
counting the scenes till he's back,

the wingflap from the crypt, the hiss,
his twisted sort of love straight through our hearts.
What is it about evil with panache

that infects, brings hot blood to the face,
makes the sullen eager, the heated crowd
all down the stairs avoid each other's eyes?

DON RODGERS

Moontan

What more pure, more lovely than a moontan?
On moonlit nights, I lie outstretched
on the lounger by the garden pool,
where the silver light sifts softly with the fish
in the cooling depths of water.

The shadows of the shrubs make boulders on the lawn
the moonlight washes round in sibilant silence.
Here there is no brash stupidity of brawn,
just the sweet exquisite scent of honeysuckle
sipped out of pale flowers by moths —

they drift like feathers in the breeze
that infiltrates the branches and the leaves.
While daylight is a place of noisy expiration,
night's the time when inspiration's filtered through
                                        the dark
and gleams. The body's colours fade to pallor,

fade and fade towards a pale perfection.
A moontanned body's incorporeal, sinless, made of soul,
a mirage glimmering in-between dark trees.
I feel my hair grow white,
as night after night it's bathed in moonlight;

my skin grows soft, with a young girl's pearly lustre,
grossness gone on a slowly ebbing tide.
Tonight the moon is full,
Her loveliness disclosed for those who see;
and I can hear a voice that murmurs from the moon,

that smoothes away all dirt, all pain,
all ruffles of vexation; a voice so soft
it makes the bushes shimmer with faint dreams;
it says: *this is my darling, my beloved,*
in whom, by whom, with whom I am well pleased.

27

The Suffering of Fishes

The suffering of fishes is childlike, naive.
Spontaneous stigmata burst at their surface
like giggles; while they wriggle: an inaudible
bodily gabble about an incredible pain.

They have, we think, affinities with things:
with shiny stones, or toys. They mostly live
in graceful quiet, the way plants do;
even when they're hauled out of the water,

don't vocalize: but twitch, like severed
tongues; and provide their own prolonged applause
the length of time it takes their flames to clog:
dying, my dear, to dephlogisticate the air.

For the suffering of fishes just ain't serious,
any more than that of jumping beans:
watch those red herrings get into a flap:
clap clap, clap clap, clap clap....

Afterwards, peruse them on the counter: wares
arranged in lines like songs, or sleek shoes.
Look them in the eye: some stare ice-bright;
but most are opaque with belatedly jaded innocence.

Mariposa

A trembling begins in the pale petals, as
the rosy pupa splits, and convulses.
"Mariposa. Mariposa," says the mouth.
The freshly articulated syllables flounce
off; flirt with meaning's draggled edge;
are caught in the pages of the foreign foliage.

The Big Battalions

After a day within Nelson's commanding reach,
erect in his concrete field with its church,
trooping out of Trafalgar in their harried lines,
marching through Waterloo's Victory Arch,
the commuters conquer a seat on the train
with their attaché cases; wearily strip
their superfluous armour off; and slump.

Newspaper shields lie over their bodies;
lances of sunlight shiver on stories;
as they pull past the corners of the Kwik Fit depot;
obliviously rattle past the fallen lorries,
the playing fields dotted with dandelion clocks,
the racecourse starting gates, the sharpened spires,
the starlings unevenly distributed on wires.

They are heading towards a renaissant future
of green and pleasant, meritocratic cloisters;
the little vicissitudes of lawns and leaves:
pristine, impervious, picturesque, prayed for —
it's there on the horizon, in the south-east;
where the Christian sun never sets, just droops,
like a Uccello orange, over the battened roofs.

Wolf-whistling for One

You're no churl:
you're far too wise to whistle at a girl.

Instead, for years,
your own sagacity's hooted in your ears.

But soon, one night,
riled, lividly rising in canescent light,

you'll silence that owl:
your wild face lifting moonlike in a howl.

Burry Holm

Sitting cross-legged on a cliff on Burry Holm,
open to the wind and the wide sea,
faced with the endlessly modulating greys,
you point in delight at the fulmars
that are planing past on their stiff wings.

Southward, the Worm is pulling strongly out to sea,
but held by the tail's still stationary.
The jagged curves of surf in Rhossili bay,
the concussive circles of the waves,
repeat their indefinite invasions of the beach.

While the ragged discs of the golden lichen Xanthoria,
encrusting the cliff like memorial Celtic suns,
emblazon echoes on the stones. You run
your hands over the radiant Braille of their faces.
"Don't you see" you say, as you sway in the west wind,

"the blinding sun that shines beyond the greys?"

Tycoch

I saw, when you said it, a house on a hill
as red as a dragon, holding in thrall
the anglicized semis and estates, that blenched
at the mighty name of "Tycoch", like vassals
cowering before its mythic magnificence.
But when I got on the bus in the Quadrant,

the driver couldn't understand my accent,
and asked me: "Is it Tea Coke you meant?"
Thus I discovered our new home was called
after colonial beverages. Nodding my assent,
I repeated after the teacher: "Coke and Tea";
and tendered him an inexact image of the Queen.

PAUL HENRY

For X and Y

God love the zimmer-frame,
the Social Worker's absorbent smile,
the hand-rail, detachable limb,
smoke-alarm, peep-hole,
the nest egg, the ancient fruit
still caught by Titan's chariot
in X and Y's maisonette,
the spats and the flimsy white hat.

God love their sallow babies
tucked away in a cradled bag,
the melanotic leaf on a bough
about to snap, the oblique wig,
bread and wine on wheels, the prayer,
the Dental Technician's pride, the crust,
the limpet-like corn plaster,
the seaside town Chiropodist.

God love the adapted plug,
the bath tub's elevating chair,
the cure for heartburn, the box of figs
unopened since 1964,
the sleeping pills, the rack of pipes,
the one tot of sherry, the lie.
God love the flutter, the papers,
the reading glass and the new sky.

God love the Daycare Nurse,
the old songs, the incontinent tales,
the monologues and the listeners,
the rain that brings out the snails.
God love the hearing aid —
THE HEARING AID! — the view of the bay,
their shells and their sugary blood,
their stitches in time, their silver days.

And God love the wedding they wore,
that hangs in a blind must,

                              that waits
for a hand on the difficult door
and then

            for a chime of light.

The Last Throws of Summer

*"Many throwers positively resent the intrusion
of a scientific explanation, preferring to keep
the magic unsullied...."*
Dr. Robert Reid (author: *The Physics of Boomerangs*)

Open-mouthed, my sister's children
cram the small bay window
at the top of the Y.H.A. — on the beach
the British Boomerang Champion
from the floor below
is justifying the autographs
such notoriety demands.

All day he's gone out
(and, true to form, come back)
to move his car a fraction,
never quite content with its place.

In the dusk his crooked wand

                              vanishes
then reappears in his hand.

What choreographs his absurd dance
carves the boomerang tide's
endlessly perfected curve,
surfs the subtle air waves
between craft and technique.
His wife screams down to him at nine
and dutifully he returns.

32

Tomorrow he'll lay his loves
in sheaths, on a childless back seat,
reverse a final one hundred degrees
and leave, less icon than nagged librarian.

And my sister's eldest will gaze
at already fading parchments,
his lightweight signatures in the sand.

Lines Written Outside a "Replica of a Sunshine Home for Blind Babies", Aberystwyth.

Did no one take a brick to this glass case?
   A ball and chain?
Now I'm old enough to press my face
   to the brittle pane

without their ghostly hugs around my gaze
   it comes home —
how time's a shell of the snail it was,
   a smaller room.

What miniature, sunken eyes remain look out
   from a pantheon
that keeps this town's unstable light,
   as I look in,

trying to read the Braille of the years between,
   with no clear sign
but, conjured back and fore by the sun,
   their faces in mine.

Welsh Incident

(In the early hours of September 3rd, 1997, a giant
turtle was found dead, on the shoreline at Criccieth.)

The Cambrian News reporter's car
blocks the lane down to the shore.

Someone plays the bagpipes
where the last field meets the sea.

But for the randomness of the tide
she'd still be gracing the waters
of a century as it drowned.

Armour-plated, run aground,
a creaturely grief mourns her end.

Two elderly, village paparazzi
circle the wreckage, take snaps
before the oceanographers descend.

Newport East

The booths close in two hours.
Ice-cream vans are on overtime.
Twinkle, twinkle... Arthur Scargill's
voice passes down the hill.
"...The only TRUE Socialist candidate..."
is addressing the slow sunset,
fathoms deeper by the word.
The town's coral gathers about them —
the sun and Arthur Scargill,
going down together,
one gracefully, one burning still.

Slipping on Leaves
(for D)

The women behind the ochre screen
weren't trying on your clothes
but slipping on leaves.

Their gentle, bearded husbands
cupped pipes like unhatched eggs,
nursed aviaries of screams
that flew in and out of their chins.

We heard the backward clocks
go tock-tock-tock....
and felt the cut of the moment.

The market's sky-blue din
tuned in like a public baths
to a swimmer cracking the surface,
a hedgerow to a beak
ticking its way through a shell.

Someone smashed the woodturner's bowl.
Glued back, varnished over
so the fissure hardly showed,
like love, it still sold.

You waved to The Wicker Man
each time his beer gut snagged
against our stall.

                    I took out the ring
from my ear and, prepossessed,
slipping on love, eased it
along your finger

                    pausing a second
at the widest joint, the hip

before pushing it all the way.

The Slipped Leash

It sways from a branch out the back
and from it hangs a nut cage.

The handstrap still whiffs of him
for all the wind and rain —
sea dog, country dog.

What misfits we'd have made,
haunting this town's streets,
our walks cut into neat
desperate portions of breath.

Now he's free and I stay in

and the nut cage swings
with winter at its wire

and someone else's dog barks.

Boys

I need them, to muscle in on this silence,
to measure the softening tissue in my arms
when I carry them up to their beds,
when the old house creaks like a galleon
after a storm.

Set adrift on their dreams
their faces turn soft again.
So that one kiss carries the weight
of all we try to make light of.

GWYNETH LEWIS

Pentecost

The Lord wants me to go to Florida.
I shall cross the border with the mercury thieves,
as foretold in the faxes and prophecies,
and the checkpoint angel of Estonia
will have alerted the uniformed birds
to act unnatural and distract the guards

so I pass unhindered. My glossolalia
shall be my passport — I shall taste the tang
of travel on the atlas of my tongue —
salt Poland, sour Denmark and sweet Vienna
and all men in the Spirit shall understand
that, in His wisdom, the Lord has sent

a slip of a girl to save great Florida.
I'll tear through Europe like a standing flame,
not pausing for long, except to rename
the occasional city; in Sofia
thousands converted and hundreds slain
in the Holy Spirit along the Seine.

My life is your chronicle; O Florida
revived, look forward to your past
and prepare your perpetual Pentecost
of golf course and freeway, shopping mall and car
so the fires that are burning in the orange groves
turn light into sweetness and the huddled graves

are hives of the future — an America
spelt plainly, translated in the Everglades
where palm fruit hang like hand grenades
ready to rip whole treatises of air.
Then the S in the tail of the crocodile
will make perfect sense to the bibliophile

who will study this land, his second Torah.
All this was revealed. Now I wait for the Lord
to move heaven and earth to send me abroad
and fulfil His bold promise to Florida.
As I stay put, He shifts His continent:
Atlantic closes, the sheet of time is rent.

The Hedge

With hindsight, of course, I can see that the hedge
was never my cleverest idea
and that bottles of vodka are better not wedged

like fruit in its branches, to counter fears
and shakes in the morning on the way to work.
Looking back, I can see how I pushed it too far

when I'd stop in the lay-by for a little lurk
before plunging my torso in, shoulder high
to the hedgerow's merciful root-and-branch murk

till I'd felt out my flattie and could drink in the dry
and regain my composure with the cuckoo-spit.
Then, with growing wonder, I'd watch the fungi,

lovely as coral in the aqueous light.
Lovely, that is, till that terrible day
when the hedge was empty. Weakened by fright

I leant in much deeper to feel out which way
the bottle had rolled and, cursing my luck
(hearing already what my bosses would say

about my being caught in this rural ruck),
I started to panic, so I tussled and heaved
and tried to stand upright, but found I was stuck.

I struggled still harder, but you'd scarcely believe
the strength in a hedge that has set its mind
on holding a person in its vice of leaves

and this one was proving a real bind.
With a massive effort, I took the full strain
and tore up the hedgerow, which I flicked up behind

me, heavy and formal as a wedding train.
I turned and saw, to my embarrassment,
that I'd pulled up a county with my new-found mane,

which was still round my shoulders, with its tell-tale scent
of loam and detritus, while trunk roads and streams
hung off me like ribbons. It felt magnificent:

minerals hidden in unworked seams
shone like slub silver in my churned-up trail.
I had brooches of newly built housing schemes

and sequins of coruscating shale;
power-lines crackled as they changed their course
and woodsmoke covered my face like a veil.

Only then did I feel the first pangs of remorse.
Still, nobody'd noticed so, quickly, I knelt,
took hold of the landscape, folded and forced

it up to a chignon which I tied with my belt.
It stayed there, precarious. The occasional spray
of blackthorn worked loose, but I quickly rebuilt

the ropey construction and tucked it away.
Since then I've become quite hard to approach:
I chew mints to cover the smell of decay

which is with me always. Food tastes of beech
and I find that I have to concentrate
on just holding the hairstyle since it's started to itch

and the people inside it are restless of late.
Still, my tresses have won me a kind of renown
for flair and I find my hair titillates

certain men who want me to take it down
in front of them, slowly. But with deepening dread
I'm watching my old self being overgrown

while scruples rustle like quadrupeds,
stoat-eyed, sharp-toothed in my tangled roots
(it's so hard to be human with a hedge on your head!).

Watch me. Any day I'll be bearing fruit,
sweet hips that glint like pinpricks of blood
and my dry-land drowning will look quite cute

to those who've never fallen foul of wood.
But on bad days now I see nothing but hedge,
my world crazed by the branches of should,

for I've lost all centre, have become an edge
and though I wear my pearls like dew
I feel that I've paid for my sacrilege

as I wish for my autumn with its broader view.
But for now I submit. With me it will die,
this narrowness, this slowly closing eye.

from Welsh Espionage

V

Welsh was the mother tongue, English was his.
He taught her the body by fetishist quiz,
father and daughter on the bottom stair:
"Dy benelin yw *elbow*, dy wallt di yw *hair*,

chin yw dy ên di, *head* yw dy ben."
She promptly forgot, made him do it again.
Then he folded her *dwrn* and, calling it fist,
held it to show her knuckles and wrist.

"Let's keep it from Mam, as a special surprise.
Lips are *gwefusau*, *llygaid* are eyes."
Each part he touched in their secret game
thrilled as she whispered its English name.

The mother was livid when she was told.
"We agreed, no English till four years old!"
She listened upstairs, her head in a whirl.
Was it such a bad thing to be Daddy's girl?

Advice on Adultery

The first rule is to pacify the wives
if you're presented as the golden hope
at the office party. You're pure of heart,
but know the value of your youthful looks.
Someone comments on your lovely back.
Talk to the women, and avoid the men.

In work they treat you like one of the men
and soon you're bored with the talk of the wives
who confide in you about this husband's back,
or that husband's ulcer. They sincerely hope
you'll never have children... it ruins your looks.
And did you know David has a dicky heart?

You go to parties with a beating heart,
start an affair with one of the men.
That fact you've been taking more care of your looks
doesn't escape the observant wives
who stare at you sourly. Cross your fingers and hope
that no one's been talking behind your back.

41

A trip to the Ladies. On your way back
one of them stops you for a heart to heart.
She hesitates, then expresses the hope
that you won't take offence, but men will be men,
and a young girl like you, with such striking looks....
She's heard nasty rumours from some of the wives.

She knows you're innocent, but the wives,
well, jump to conclusions from the way it looks....
In a rage you resolve she won't get him back,
despite the pressure from the other wives.
They don't understand... you'll stick with the men,
only they are *au fait* with affairs of the heart.

You put it to him that you're living in hope.
He grants that you're beautiful, but looks
aren't everything. He's told the men,
who smirk and wink. So now you're back
to square one, but with a broken heart.
You make your peace with the patient wives.

Don't give up hope at the knowing looks.
Get your own back, have a change of heart:
Ignore the men, start sleeping with the wives.

from Zero Gravity

I. Prologue

We watched you go
in glory: Shuttle,
comet, sister-in-law.

The one came back.
The other two
went further. Love's an attack

on time. The whole damn thing
explodes, leaving
us with our count-down days

42

still more than zero.
My theme is change.
My point of view

ecstatic. See how speed
transforms us? Didn't you know
that time's a fiction? We don't need

it for travel. Distance
is a matter of seeing;
faith, a science

of feeling faint objects.
Of course, this is no
consolation as we watch you go

on your dangerous journeys.
This out of mind
hurts badly when you're left behind.

Don't leave us.
We have more to say
before the darkness. Don't go. Stay

a little longer. But you're out of reach
already. Above us the sky
sees with its trillion trillion eyes.

III

It looks like she's drowning
in a linen tide.
They bring babies like cameras
to her bedside

because they can't see dying.
She looks too well
to be leaving. She listens
to anecdotes we tell —

43

how we met and got married.
She recounts a story:
her friend went stark mad
carrying, feeding, bleeding — all three

at once. She tried to bury
herself in Barry Island sand.
Her prayer plant has flowered
after seven years. She sends

Robert to fetch it from System St.
She thinks a bee sting
started the cancer.
We can't say a thing.

V

First time I saw the comet, I finally knew
that I'd always love him. I watched it go,

dead starlight headed for a dying sun
then away into darkness. It was gone

before we knew what its brilliance meant,
a human moment in immense

spirals of nothing. I feel his pull
in my blood salts. The comet's tail

is a searchlight from another point,
and the point is once you've given your heart

there are no replacements. Oh, your soul,
if that can escape from its own black hole.

VI

Last suppers, I fancy, are always wide-screen.
I see this one in snapshot: your brothers are rhymes
with you and each other. John has a shiner
from surfing. Already we've started counting time
backwards to zero. The Shuttle processed
out like an idol to its pagan pad.
It stands by its scaffold, being tended and blessed
by priestly technicians. You refuse to feel sad,
can't wait for your coming wedding with speed
out into weightlessness. We watch you dress
in your orange space suit, a Hindu bride,
with wires like henna for your loveliness.
You carry your helmet like a severed head.
We think of you as already dead.

VII

Thousands arrive when a bird's about to fly,
crowding the causeways. "Houston. Weather is a go
and counting." I pray for you as you lie
on your back facing upwards. A placard shows
local, Shuttle and universal time.
Numbers run out. Zero always comes.
"Main engines are gimballed" and I'm
not ready for this, but clouds of steam
billow out sideways and a sudden spark
lifts the rocket on a collective roar
that comes from inside us. With a sonic crack
the spaceship explodes to a flower of fire
on the scaffold's stamen. We sob and swear,
helpless, but we're lifting a sun
with our love's attention, we hear
the Shuttle's death rattle as it overcomes
its own weight with glory, setting car alarms
off in the Keys and then it's gone
out of this time zone, into the calm
of black and we've lost the lemon dawn
your vanishing made. At the viewing site
we pick oranges for your missing light.

STEPHEN KNIGHT

The Big Parade

Here they come past High Street station, everyone I've ever known
and some I've only seen on television, marching three abreast,

my Junior School Headmistress at the front — Miss Morgan
with her bosoms now as much a shelf as when I saw her last

it must be thirty years ago — hurling to the sky a silver baton
(twirling up it tumbles earthwards like the prehistoric bone

in Kubrick's *2001*): turning at the Dizzy Angel Tattoo Studio
down Alexandra Road then into Orchard Street they go,

my other teachers — Grunter, Crow and Mister Piss on stilts —
juggle furry pencil-cases, worn board-dusters, power balls,

there's Adam West, his Batman outfit taut around his waist,
and then the Monkees, Mickey hammering a drum the others

blowing on kazoos: they navigate the Kingsway roundabout
to pass the Odeon where everyone is dropping ticker-tape

a storm of paper falls on Malcolm in a stripey tank-top, John
and Hugh and catches in the hairnet of our loony neighbour

Nestor — keeping up despite an ancient Zimmer frame —
and Bill the communist and Mister Shaddick, hirer of skips,

his brown bell-bottoms crack and snap around his platform shoes,
the collar of his paisley-patterned shirt's two giant set squares

look! a girl from Pennsylvania who kissed me once, still thirteen
after twenty years, I shouldn't recognise her smile and yet I do,

I call to her but she's too far away, atop a jewelled elephant
she's waving to the crowd like someone fresh from outer space:

travelling along St Helen's Road towards the sea, the cheers,
the noises of the instruments resounding through the city centre

out, past vinyl three-piece suites and lava lamps in Eddershaws
go Mary Dorsett, Julie Dolphin, Tony (very much alive),

Rhiannon then a row of faces I can't put a name to now
but still I wave and shout and watch them disappear,

the boy who butted me one break-time skulking at the back,
the music fading, blurring with the gulls, the sea, the sounds

of people going home, till everywhere I look
the streets are quiet as a fall of snow.

After Lessons

The classrooms are as dead as winter trees.
You hold your breath along the corridor —
Your plimsolls creak. There is no other noise.

A single light ices the polished floor.
You turn and, somehow, end up in The Boys,
A row of basins level with your knees.

You shouldn't be inside this place so late.
I wonder what you thought you might achieve
By squinting at the blackboard. What, and how?

In the dark, you wipe your nose across your sleeve.
It's much too late to put your hand up now.
There's someone outside, waiting at the gate.

The Desert Inn

Sand is at the door,
Its progress through the keyhole slow:
I raise both hands to hold it back before

Sand inches, grain by grain, along the hallway floor:
Among the slippers, dunes begin to grow:
Sand is at the door

Of every cupboard, every drawer
Brims, postcards on the mantelpiece no longer show:
I raise both hands to hold it back before

My deepest rooms become extensions of the shore:
Now, where the goldfish used to come and go
Sand is: at the door,

In books, on pillows, more and more
Sand pours towards me: with one, whispered "no"
I raise both hands to hold it back before

My waist, my chest, my neck, my jaw
And mouth succumb to sand, its undertow...
Sand is at the door...
I raise both hands to hold it back before

Elvis

He's out there somewhere, in the dark —
a pair of oil-stained overalls,
a monkey wrench. When drivers park
to stretch their legs and scratch their balls

he appears with a chamois leather
in a pail of suds. He doesn't pass
the time of night, curse the weather
nor laugh; he only cleans the glass.

Bored, tired from counting off the states
they've spanned, they can't see how odd
he is, the man who never talks;

the tubby, balding guy who waits
for tips, then shrugs.
                    The one who walks
across the forecourt like a god.

The Mermaid Tank

Beneath my weight, the duckboards bow.
    Two buckets, slopping water, weigh me down.
A cold wind howls around the cages now,
    While rain sweeps in — across the town —
Again; and while our rheumy-eyed,
    Arthritic monsters fall asleep
        Or vegetate
            I kneel beside
The Songstress Of The Deep
    And wait.

All afternoon, the punters pass
    Her tank in single file; because it's dark
Inside, they press their faces to the glass.
    I breathe, at night, on every mark.
Behind my cloth, the water churns
    And curls around our fat dugong
        And when it clears
            (Like smoke) she turns
Away, and any song
    I hear

Is "just the wind" or "my mistake"....
    Outside, discarded handbills catch their wings
On tents or in the mud while, in their wake,
    Paper cups, ticket stubs and things
The rain dismantles every night
    Turn cartwheels in the foreign air

Before they throng
   The sky, too light
To settle anywhere
  For long.

So Early in the Year

*(Presumably the whole point is that there should be
no continuum: of anything. That failures of memory
are but a proof of a living organism's subordination
to the laws of nature. No life is meant to be preserved.)*
   —Joseph Brodsky: *In a Room and a Half.*

"I really ought to stop
climbing trees," you said,
nipping the filter off
another low-tar cigarette
then settling your arm
lightly on my shoulder,
giving me a squeeze
as if you didn't know
that you were dead.

— THUMP THUMP
thumpthumpthump...
The builder opposite
plays Capital all day.
His hammer in the air,
a nail between his teeth,
he dances,
dances like a little boy
till everything's OK.

The Green, fluorescent
after rain, is buzzing,
with ZIPPOS' grimy
Day-Glo trailers
scattered like toys.

While men lug rope,
funambulists in tights
pitch in, or practise
death-defying feats.

You looked quite wrong —
your eyes too far apart,
your hair too long
and coppery — and yet
the way in dreams
we know, I knew
(deep down) that it
was you, knee-deep
in reams of leaves.

The golden chain tree's
flowers blew away
so early in the year,
now wizened seedpods
hang above the path,
but they're juggling fire
out there, balancing —
on long broom-handles
— children, who throw

their arms out wide.

ANNA WIGLEY

Boxing Day to Lidney

After the night's slow
tempera of crystal and flake

laying layers of silence
white on white,

the valley is painted
at shoulder and hip:

a voluptuously sequinned
starlet in Versace.

The quiet has gathered in clumps
on the paw-pads of firs,

sprayed stones with salt,
laid a line of white

on the meanest twig.
By dawn the birches are carved

Japanese sculptures of ice,
silver-scarved necks

rustling heads of lace.
The fields are white lakes

of coconut milk
below an acre of blue

with the lid blown off.
Under the trees at noon

shadows lay
small black knives.

The Last Cobbler in Canton

His hands are broad as a gorilla's,
the fingernails sunk rivet-deep.
He flips my boots like fillets of beef,
judging the cut,
then paring the heels of fat.

His wheels are dragged up
from some forge by Bosch:
millstones that spin and spark.
Stealing fire, planing off,
he swings between turbine and shelf,
pulling the tacks like teeth.

Tuned to the moods of tar and wood,
knowing the shoe's skeleton
with one loving stroke, he daubs
and smelts the heel's scalloped moon
to a seamless mould.

And nothing in his rough-cut face
is surprised or proud
at this ten-minute miracle, violent
and precise as a surgeon's tailoring
or a hawk's death-swoop.

Duck-shooting

That was the summer you took me
on gunmetal mornings, early,
to strange deserted places:

wet ground, forests of rushes,
hard grass stubbling
from a sodden mattress.

Mindful of my privilege
I was silent as instructed,
trod softly in the wake

of your long legs and galoshes.
In the holster of your hip
the butt of your rifle jogged.

Toads the colour of mud
panted silently on mud ledges.
We caught the electric trace

of a snake. No wind.
Just a cold smell of water
and the sky getting lower.

On a jigsaw of cracked sludge
you crooked a knee,
patted me down, slid the catch;

I saw nothing but the back of your head
as you leaned like a cat
into the eye of the sight,

clenching yourself round the gun
until you had it tamed,
and with a slow squeeze let death out.

The ducks were soft and loose
as bundles of silk.
Their rainbowed necks

lolled from the mouth of your bag.
Later we would pick the shot
from the stopped hearts

be soldierly and not mind
the sick tug of quills from flesh,
the high bier of feathers.

Big Weekend

A bass vibration in the street.
Lasers twirling a faint wheel
of low stars. Top slice
of a dipper, tips of shrieks.

Lads and their girls
peel off from the scene
like boxers from the ring,
punch-drunk on shakers,
rodeos, big swings;
sloshed on volcanic tea,
fingers vinegar-perfumed.

Young toughs walk the waltzers
like sailors on a stormy deck,
make pay-up signs
as they straddle the troughs,
flip coins like apes
gulping nuts, then spin
with one finger the wailing cars.

Braced for the plunge
into almost-death,
young women's stomachs swim
to have stepped so lightly
into such cheap heroism,
risking all, risking nothing
in the bought fall's
crimson thrill.

SAMANTHA WYNNE RHYDDERCH

The Lighthouse Keeper's Daughter

was the first to see the dead musician's
eyes at dawn, blue and immense

as Llangorse Lake where his voice
would echo from water to rock to

water. That was before the migraines
bleached her tongue, combing her skull

each night until mute with pain she
polished cobalt vowels in the wind.

The whiteness throbbed round
and round, firm and eternal as

this glass tower, a prism
practising madness: light, limb, dark,

blade, light, clover, dark, lake, light,
dark, wound, dark, dark.

The X-Ray Room

I am dismantled in monochrome
on the screen opposite the student doctors,
their gaze moving from me here to

me translated into porcelain
there. I am Exhibit A, my symmetry
unmasked by this cut and paste version

of my guts hermeneutically sealed
in negative. I stand by my parallel
text as if to elucidate

evisceration. My bones
in triplicate have nowhere to hide.
Their fragility becomes heraldic

when these exegetes invoke them
in Latin. You see, my other
has been deceiving me all along.

Pope Gregory XI's Bedroom

He has rhyming wallpaper
with parakeets on green tendrils.
Over his bed stretch

ostrich feathers arching
into a dome he dreams he'll see again
one day, down south.

From his stone windowsill he'll
fit a convent in his ring
where six pray daily in their cells

that he won't choke on quails
or lose his throne to some Italian
jerk. He muses on how best to

silence her, that odd Dominican who
writes continually, insisting that he
give it up, come back to Rome.

At night he crushes eggshells between his teeth,
sees the Rhône swirling below,
deep, filled with his own blood, slow.

Lighting the Fire

Temperamental, I know you will do nothing until
your bed is made up. I give you one match, like a word
and you will talk all evening. You take possession
of my jewels as you draw yourself up. You want them all
for yourself and I let you, with my raw dependence on heat.
You eat and eat as if you have some rare disease.
You're an addiction in yourself — I could stay by your side
all night. If I placed no limits on you, I know you'd
take over the whole house. You're so demanding
you and your dust; yet I fall for you every time,
the unregimented smell of chopped pine
in the grate.

The Phonebook Errata

This is a recorded message
from BT: we'd like to apologise for
omitting all the bachelors this year.

So these are the ones who got away —
the undialled, the deleted, the disconnected,
the illegible, the eligible who ticked the wrong box,
foxed BT with an odd surname
or an unpronounceable address.
They didn't expect to be
ex-directory. It was a free gift after
they became temporarily unavailable.
All those digits losing their
touch in drawers remain
unbilled, lineless, unobtainable,
constantly hung up. Perhaps they'll
get a better reception next year.

If you find yourself in any way
affected by this error, we advise you
to press your star button twice
now.

58

The Breakdown

(for David Helfgott)

I emerge from the velvet drapes
like a king. The piano is ready,
black and polished as a coffin.
I want to climb into its open back
and pull the lid down, but I know
it will not swallow me whole. My torture
is to be of a different kind — note by note until
there is no more sound, only the flat tapping
of someone trying to get me out.

I sit at the keyboard
imagining the seascape I am to
sculpt from these black and white blocks.
All the violins turn to me like arrows.
The silence tightens
as if a gunman had centred his target.
I nod and begin. My fingers tantalize
the keys. A string is cut. I am free.
I give my soul to the notes. It is perfect.
I take off, feet folded in, wings whole and flowing.
Below me the tigers smile. They want
my bones, but I am going higher and higher.
I am with the notes. They will not catch me,
the tigers in their suits below.

I do not recognise the movement
of those hands. They are so taut and raw.
I'm up in the dome. Below
they are mesmerised. I hear nothing but
flat tapping on wet keys. At the crescendo I zoom
into the fingers as if they are gloves.
It is the end. I stand. There is clapping. My head
hits the lid. A light goes out. The orchestra bends
over me like a group of designated mourners.

White, white, green. The Rach III. Free,
in a white gown. Who are these, the green-masked
who tie me down, thread strings through my skin,
their instruments off key in metal bowls?
Are they playing the Rach III on me? Did I
crash into the dome on the way up
and out? Perhaps the tigers sank their teeth
in too deep. Am I to be inscribed,
petrified on a page by these
whose mouths are bound?

When the white bolts shoot through
me, I am not here
on this steel bed.
I am with the notes,
up in the dome.
I am the Rach III.

The Bridesmaids' Reply

It's difficult with snorkels.
We watch your breath
effervesce: words we'll never hear
burst to the surface. Twenty foot
under, you begin to unfurl
like dried flowers, your hair wild
and static as starfish. When you laugh
at the photographer's webbed feet,
the coral waits grim-faced and decadent,
while the musicians tune up
in the bar.

ZOË SKOULDING

Trappist Brewers

They smile and glide as if time means nothing,
as if there are no billboards outside the sleepy town
showing how Chimay is drunk in Tokyo.

From their glassed-in cloisters they remember
how power, prayer and alcohol flooded the veins
of the oldest maps. The road from the abbey leads

to the town square, where the bells ring slightly
out of tune, tinny and distinct, marking out
each quarter hour while nothing changes.

Wild rabbit from the fields below melts
into plums and onions; the cheese is creamy,
dipped in salt. Remembering that rich, slow drunkenness

back home, I will buy the same beer
under bland fluorescent light
and drink it from the wrong glass,

searching its bitter velvet for a footstep on stone,
an off-key chime or a white scut
disappearing into the woods.

Eclipse

The little boxes in the café show it all in original 3D.
You fit your eyes to two round lenses in the wood,
focus, and the past sharpens. You could almost
limp into the trench with the men who carry
that shrouded body. After a moment you see
how it is missing from the chest up.

You can drive for miles through fields which still
explode each time they're ploughed, the earth
still white and heavy, clinging to your feet in lumps,
dragging you down while you stare up.

Keep watching the skies for signs and portents:
everyone knows where the future's coming from.
Families with welding shields and matching mirror specs
gaze up in one direction, B-move extras in some scene
where everybody's awe-struck in the mud, while the sun
hauls itself along with its jaw shot away.

Suddenly it all slides into perspective
as you see how far away the sun is, how black,
how next time you will be absent.

Gibraltar

The little neck of sea is difficult
for submarines to slide through undetected;
all night you dream of the drip
drip on metal, the immense pressure of water
and the eyes of the enemy.

Two continents stretch out their fingertips
but don't quite touch. We can see Africa,
we can see it clearly.

Your gaze meets mine over Guinness
in a mock-Tudor no-man's land
as warplanes scream from the TV screen.
We drain our glasses.

In a small room in a narrow lane
you steer my finger through the ring,
then we escape, blinking into sunshine.
On the empty runway we pose together
while a stranger takes a photo
and my white dress is a sail
which lifts a little in the wind.

Sledging

On his study wall that photograph
captured in its black and ivory
a memory of snow-capped ranges, vast
in the small world of a Suffolk rectory.
Annapurna, which he almost reached
(his fifties mountain jacket in the attic,
moulding) teased him all his life, bleached
bones of a desire lost in static
clouds. Or did the Himalayas hide
in other hills? I am nine years old.
My father pulls our sledge through a field as white
as loss before we plummet into cold
dizzy fear and feel a sharp wind blow.
I bury my face in his coat and smell snow.

Kraftwerk

This electrical hum is not eternal.
Tones pure as wax gather on wires,
slide into silence.

Insects hover before the storm,
their wings inaudible heartbeats.

Ghosts of machines
sing of their loss in
voices which cannot crack,
grieving over the perfect
death of the mistake.

Map

Monkeys on the roof wake us
after days of scanning empty forest
for a glimpse of silver or a halo of white fur.

Outside, we try to photograph
the arched backs, curled tails,
spring dives down into the endless green,

the miraculous landings, but they're gone
and there's nothing but a shiver of leaves.
The film is full of shots of trees.

Prakash Stores: For Everything You Need.
Yellowing in the cabinet is a map
surveyed before I was born;

New Road isn't on it but every building
is marked by name: Fairview, Cosy Nook,
St Paul's. The missionaries don't let go —

their kingdom still sits firmly on the ridge
while landslides block the roads and only monkeys
play on the crumbling tennis courts.

I trace with a finger the English cemetery
where we once sat in darkness by an open grave
and you said that life is a series of leaps

into the unknown, of which death is the last.

DERYN REES-JONES

My Father's Hair

For it has stood up like a coxcomb before a fight.
For it is whiter than lace on a bobbin or snow on a bough.
For in his youth it was auburn, leading to blackness.
For it has a grave insouciance,
What they call in Sassoon's "a natural air".
For it has resisted gels and lotions, brilliantine, mousses.
For it has been photographed, ridiculed,
Admired, swept back.
For it speaks the language of wild things, everywhere.
For it has suffered the barbary of barbers, and my mother.
For it has been tamed with deerstalkers,
Baseball and camouflage caps.
For it is something of a pirate or an admiral.
It is a spark transmitter and a Special Constable,
It is Harrier Jumpjet, parachute, Chinook.
For it is salt on an eyelash, fresh from the sea
For it is loved by many women of the district,
And is piped aboard the sternest of vessels.
For it cannot be mentioned, the pot of *Vitalis*
She gave him on their honeymoon.
For its mind is as fast as light, the elastic stretch
Of a falling star. It is not anybody's servant.
For we will say nothing of Delilah and Seville.
It is both gravel path and skating rink.
It is velvet, it is epaulettes. It is sunrise, it is sunset.
O my father's hair! It is an unsung hero!
But because of the sickness, or the cure for the sickness,
It lies like an angel's on the pillow:
Long white strands, like wings, or long white wings, like hair.

The Memory Tray

(The language game "I am afraid" already contains the object.)
— Wittgenstein

There was a milk tooth, with the string that pulled it.
There was a letter in your father's hand.
Welcome to the real world.
There was a chocolate heart wrapped in red tin foil.
There was, *embarrassment,*
A contraceptive. A sanitary towel.
There was a can of laughter.
Can you remember?

Remember I remember I remember.
There was a photograph of somebody I never knew
But knew the name of; there was a tiny paper box,
So beautiful. There was an object
That I can't quiet place.
Here instead is my dream.
I remember it in order: (1) *A big man*
(2) *with his big hands* (3) *in a maze who*
Sees (4) *a flock of birds, then,*
Stoops (5) *to tie his shoes, his fingers*
(6's and 7's) *fingering the laces sadly*
Like the drooping heads of flowers....

The One That Got Away

In the Midleton factory
Where you worked for three summers
You fell for a woman
You swore you would marry
If only for the sake
Of the tale you could tell
Years later,
About the day you met:
This doe-eyed, wide-hipped,
Inspectress of Peas, who,

Testing for sweetness, consistency,
Size — this will kill you, you said —
With the *Pea Tenderometer*,
You made jump from her skin
(Sweet Jesus, this your only sin:
To lean across her gently,
Nibble at the darted cotton apron
Covering her breasts
And whisper how you wanted her....)
And who, in fear, surprise,

Punched a perfect, pea-shaped hole
Straight through your thumb.
These days, when you hold your hand
Up to the light, squint through yourself
Like a painter, with one eye open
And one eye closed
At all the aching sky,
And start on this story
With a squeeze and a smile,
I'm still not sure.

The one that got away?
The pea-shaped flesh?
The pear-shaped girl?

What It's Like To Be Alive

(after Django Bates)

I remember the nights, and the sounds of the nights,
and the moon, and the clouds, then the clear sky

and the stars and angels on the Rye,
and I remember the way we knelt on the bed, how the
                                                    bedclothes
were a tide, and the sunlight was a tide, and how
                                        everything pulled,

and I remember the trains, leaving and arriving,
and I remember the tears, your tears, and my tears

and how we were children, not lovers,
how the angels cried,

and I remember your face and you coming in my hands,
and the clouds, and the stars, and how, for a moment,
with our eyes tight closed how the planets lurched

and the angels smiled,
and I remember how I did not know if this was grief or love,

this hot pool
and the sounds,
and then nothing.

A watermark held up to the light.
A boat rowed off the edge of the world.

Calcium

Because I love the very bones of you,
and you are somehow rooted in my bone,
I'll tell you of the seven years

by which the skeleton renews itself,
so that we have the chance to be
a person, now and then, who's

something other than ourselves;
and how the body, if deficient,
will bleed the calcium it needs —

for heart, for liver, spleen —
from bone, which incidentally,
I might add, is not the thorough

structure that you might
suppose, but living tissue which
the doctors say a woman of my age

should nurture mindfully with fruit,
weightbearing exercise, and supplements
to halt the dangers of a fracture when I'm old;

and because I love you I will also tell
how stripped of skin the papery bone
is worthy of inscription, could hold

a detailed record of a navy or a store of grain,
and how, if it's preserved
according to the pharaohs,

wrapped in bandages of coca leaf, tobacco,
it will survive long after all our books,
and even words are weightless;

and perhaps because the heaviness of your head,
the way I love the slow, sweet sense of you,
the easiness by which you're stilled,

how the fleshy structures that your skeleton,
your skull maintain, are easily interrogated,
it reminds me how our hands,

clasped for a moment, now, amount
to everything I have; how even your smile
as it breaks me up, has the quality of ice,

the long lines of loneliness
like a lifetime ploughed across a palm,
the permanence of snow.

Snow Song

All summer I've waited,
Weaving this cloth of burrs and nettles
Till my hands
Prickle and blister
Like bubbles of oxygen
Trapped under glass.

Then suddenly the snow:
Snow being born of itself,
Snow feathering your cheeks, lashes, lips,
Snow, being more than itself,
The colour of nothing.
Snow like the wings of a long-necked bird....

And I call you, whispering.
A few days is all we have.

70

FRANCES WILLIAMS

Descent

The wing can hold the curve of the earth
Tucked like a pillow under its hard arm.

Australia is passing me her endless
Biscuit prairie, patch scrub trimming off

To curly beach. Peninsulas are sharp
As holly. And then a rash of salt lakes,

A strange pox, turquoise then urine.
At such altitudes, reassurance arrives

In the small white intimacy of plastic
Meals. My cheese cracker is bigger

Than Kangaroo Island. I measure the gap
Between hand and mouth as Melbourne

Fades to Adelaide. Between safety and
Danger, a continent surrenders its widest

Plan. Its dust is the colour of strong char.
Lower, and roads criss cross in grids, run

Straight and true, hold too fast to purpose,
Are thin experiments in meaning. Out through

The bushy tail of history, my travels blow
Sky high. Wherever you go, you're only

Ever you, my mother warned me. But
There again, perhaps she had an interest

In the retardation of the coming new.
The chord at my tail frays in wispy spray,

Slowly dissolves in the long white sun
Which laces the window with its ice.

At Perth the runway beckons as the future
Swiftly rises from the past. Local time

Greets me with a roar, my head held tight
In the playful bite of world as carnivore.

Test Ahead

My first lesson. And he's balancing a diagram
On his slim green knees, showing me the flow
Of speed and power. As I move the levers to fit
My frame, I feel the bones inside my skeleton
Glow, doing their slow motions for the camera
Of a scientist measuring the distance between
Curb, child, wheel. And once we're off, it seems
That the whole street is learning to be itself again
Wide as a cinema and stroked with different signs.
I gather past vistas in my tiny bug-eared mirrors.

From the body outward, I learn to trust this shell,
Husk, wires, the spool of steel, the big divorce
Between one way of knowing and another. Touch
Of my toes prompts the whole go, stronger than
Zeus: then slow, learning a crawl of incremental
Retardation. Even as I note ten people die a day
Clocking the tiny coffins on the page, I aim for
A destination where no accidents happen. Belief
And the red circles, jumping through the hoops.

As a child asleep on the rubber smelling seat
Of the old Dolomite, the low hum of my father
Carried me, safe entirely. The man at my side

Uses his broken ball-point to make a final point:
I forget and remember the shapes my body makes,
The seat, like a lover, holding me just right.

72

The Tall Man

From flinty beaches and their crackling drags
We rode towards The Downs, aimed to meet the vacant
Gaze of the Widcombe Giant, his white rims beckoning.

He slips through trees, a thumbnail print, then reappears
Fiercer as the meadow spins our wheels faster towards
His steepening slope. He holds two sticks, long length

Of his stance. Double speared, he holds out a welcome
Or warning. Between two poles, he plants thick thighs,
Breasting the pale blue of the horizon's haze. Nearer,

And his weight lifts as we push the incline hard, his huge
Heftiness held by chalk threads, thin gravel. His big head
Is grass filled, ground etched. The habits people have

Of following old paths, digging in, of gauging out these
Snake curves of shoulder, knee, foot. The floury flints
Crunch beneath our feet as wheat fields tilt and hush

In their swung battalions. We look where he looks, lie
On the heat of the ground and feel our rims holding us
Skin under the skin, marker of our hottest tides of flesh.

The clouds pass over like the shape of breath, our ogre
Mounds humped like tumuli beneath the skylark's peep.
We lie at his feet, little children who've found their father

Wanting. Snug in the drawing of his curving heel, he's
Smaller than we thought he ever was, this hillside peeled
Like the flap of our former map. And we walk over him.

What Survives

I spiral up the Guggenheim's
Gorgeous twisted heart, looking at
Picasso: the war years. A woman

Scissors her handkerchief in a long
Concertina of pain. Her wrinkles
Cut razor deep, salty with tears. Next,

Three stump heads, the bloodied skulls
Of sheep, jangle in a three-headed
Pyramid. They are laughing, jaws

Ahoy, on jig jags of tusk. A funny bone
Tickles them, gigglers all, whose little
Teeth, right on the lip of their chins,

Stick out a drawer of the purest mischief.
Outside, the pretzel man sells his knots,

Wearing a solemn face, as though
They were equations of eternity.

Oyster Eating

Luxury doesn't get more
Astringent. Plucked from
Cloudy depths, my plate
Of oysters wait for their
Moment, little glaciers
In silky cups. I suck

An avalanche of flesh.
Then clear my throat
Of their strange salt
Swallow, more touch
Than taste. Out of these
Rocky skulls, the brains

Come slippery as sex.
Each one tips over the
Rugged callused lips of
Its single shoe to speak
Only with the one tongue,
A probe both first and

Last. Such rash
Adventurers. Jonahs
In my whale. And also
Something sad in our
Hurried consummation.
A dozen down, I reach

A check-mate moment
In this game of numbers.
As Casanova, on a lucky
Night, might break a line
Of kisses, to pause for breath
On heaven's racing staircase.

Bed Time

We lugged the old one out: stiff square
Of all my sleeps, weeping sad stains,
Humble lump of all absorption. I felt

Its bending weight thump my shoulder
Down every step. A decade of dreams,
Unremembered, in its flank, nudging

A blunt exit. And all my motives sunk
In the heat of its musk, its grey snowscape
Of skin and dust, shaken but not stirred.

Here amongst the pattern of its lines
You'll find my hopes exhausted, desires
Thwarted and fear, the colour of blue ink.

On a sea of slack this raft has swum
Its course. It buckles in the street, bent
Double to the world's exacting certainty.

The Actress

(From the film *Persona*.)

Here is the oval face of Bibi Andersson.
Her head is wide as a planet. But instead

Of craters and volcanoes, she carries
The softness of being infinitely human.

Dark moods migrate across her skin
Like lost tribes forcing a way to memory.

She's held, for a daringly long duration,
By the four-corners of Ingmar Bergman.

He smothers her with Bach, a solemn hood
Of notes, aching through light. It's 1966

And over the pores of her powdered skin
A day is ending. But something else lets

Itself in. Watching and feeling watched —
The two compete in the interrogation

Her eyes witness and rival. The sun still
Abandons Scandinavia as it stole away from

Bergman and the crew who might surround
Her like the Magi, intent, perhaps, and listening.

The score was later stripped, over the action,
To create the exact moment, journeying still,
That now passes through itself, like an eclipse.

FIONA SAMPSON

Pastoral from a Millennial Pattern Book

The nuns' cows are coming, all porcelain
ornament and exquisite movement,
down the East Hayfield;

a hatch clatters in the notched oak;
birds slip with soft
tearing sounds through superheated air.

Sea-shadows below this field are like stains:
signs, not meant,
of deepening reality

where we float
among the white tossed
clover, cultivate our cares.

— And after the Millennium, what remains?
Or what's here now? For this scene's only lent
— it's got an eighteenth-century feel —

from a pattern-book;
and every pastoral returns to loss,
cow-like, with conscientious care.

The Misunderstanding

Those lilies. The space they took.
Now I understand how they flared into life
each lifted lip creamy and abundant
each trumpet a blare of money. Vulgar with optimism

I picked them from their bucket
in a shop where two men were teaching
a labrador tricks. The shady interior
prickled with cellophane.

On the shelf, on your shelf, the birthday lilies
magnetised the light from the lamps
in an autocracy of the sexy.
They seemed a pivot, a vacuum

of all that might happen next
or had. For you they were already
hardening, an image of light and of white
like new walls, a place that might turn out

to be sudden and generous as an Israeli flower
out of the badlands of history
out of dark interiors, a bolt of beauty
with nothing but salvation in mind.

I'd no idea. I sat watching the flowers
drink the light. They were packed with it.
They were a lightshow lasering over and
over extravagant blank cursives.

The X File

It doesn't matter what I say or do,
You don't love me. That's the end of it.
Doesn't matter that I loved so well
I lost myself in keeping sight of you.
No gifts, no words, no tendernesses prove
Truths that you untell, the proofs you fell
Blind to logic, making stories fit
The way your shoulder used to, or the tender groove
Between your thumb and palm that once clipped mine
Neat as a file, holding knowledge tight:
That you were mine. You're not tonight.
Instead I travel on, through dark so fine
You might think that was what got in my eyes:
And not the strain of saying these goodbyes.

Legal and Tender

When the telephone rings unexpectedly or my neighbour
ties her dogs to the gatepost and comes in
to talk about the buyer she just got
or I'm in the bath and add things up:

what comes to mind's
people with lives that are legal and tender,
that they can keep warm in their hands. Petals
on the porch floor, colour photographs

with everyone in frame, food
only an afterthought and (we're British) really
not that much to get excited over.
And in the park their kids kicking a ball

each foot landing right, while overhead
the punctual planes come safely in, rain falls
in punctuating well-anticipated showers and everything
is natural without end right to the end.

from Green Thought

Stealthy as any unicorn he
drops his capsule among the books:
knowing that unreason, like ink, runs
the more you rub at it.

Inexpungeable, alert, with muddied fingers
poised like a chef's, he
sows the brilliant flowers
that hedge the child's dreams

and pout in the dreams
of her parents. The readers sleep.
Poetry jumps ship from her shelf
and stalks into the moonlight:

79

she's the songster and the bloodied
shroud. Our heroine
clenches her hand to the bedhead again:
sweet Jack, nimble Jack's come calling.

About the House

Nothing added or taken away, nothing slipping
                                    through words
as if it should be there, a captured beast:
no stalls, no stableyard, no horsebox
to do a turn in, no nuzzling sounds in the dark

even when we aren't there. Nothing's proximate,
what doesn't live under cover isn't open either.
The windows of the house are open to the Westerly:
haze, sun, a couple of toppling kittens

and the neighbour's dog driving itself wild
with its own echo. But nothing comes in.
No comprehensive palliative word
comes in like an embrace; the skin of no meaning

touches my arm below the sleeve.
The trees talk only to themselves
and the words signal back: branch, drop.
Summer goes on adding to itself, day after day.

SARAH CORBETT

Dream of a Horse

Rushes of breath in the dark —
at my face something is hot,
picking out pores in the skin.
Beneath my hands a belly heaves,
a trellis of veins steaming under silk.

A hoof strikes —
once, twice, the ground thundering.
A concurrence of tone and force
repeats through a puzzle of bone:
a long thigh against my hip, my breast to a sickle
of rib.

It shifts balance, muscle clenched,
unclenched, remembering the taste of steel,
an insistence: at the mouth, hard at its flank —
the give and fold of neck,
the shoulder's force like water.

Around us, taking up the slack,
the air is sparse, sharp
to the sudden angle of an ear,
an eye rolling back its white
to catch sight of what it can smell.

My Mother's Lover

My mother has a new lover.
He shovels the clutter from her head
like the coalman, heaps of hot stone
clattering beneath the house;
leaves before we awake.

She says he soothes her,
the palm of her right hand complaining
against the crook of her spine.
I imagine him smearing the heat of his olive skin
across her back, burning.

Last night she let me taste her lipstick,
tacky dabs of mauve on my mouth.
She talked of his fine hands,
the fingers with their bulbous tips,
how they make you shiver, electric.

I could see him, putting his finger
to her tongue, causing the lights
under the closed lids to jump and spark;
she showed me too how they kissed,
putting her electric tongue to mine and giggling.

The Red Wardrobe

The red wardrobe where you shut in my sister,
the iron key sliding into your pocket.

The red wardrobe that fell on my sister,
its colour old blood and rusty oil
on the soft blue insides of her elbows, her wrists,

like the Chinese burns she gave me
as I cried and hated her, until I remembered
how she made herself small in corners,
how I thought she was a kitten crying until I shook her.

The red wardrobe, its doors opening and closing in
                                        my dream,
the warm nuts in its dust becoming mice eyes,
their long tails, scratching,

that my father splintered and burnt
the day all the women left and we had fireworks.

Letter to a Lover

I am sending you my heart,
it will be my messenger,
a hummingbird singing at a flower.

Isn't this beautiful, what you have of me?
Does it still beat against its sides,
is it breathless?

Does it hold its colour —
of my night-long forays under the skin,
the inside burgundy of tulips?

It is a beetle, armoured and glistening.
If you put your finger to it
it will split and spread wings.

An impatient creature,
it has guessed that you think of me,
the ridge of my hip, my belly's henge.

Here I am, a nail
finding its place under my breast,
a slate of bone prised into my palm.

Riding The Waves To Bring You Home

These horses wreck themselves on the black shore,
hammer their limbs at the sea-gates.
I cut my body on scarred muscle,
at my waist your anchor rope.

My voice is taken in anger, this recklessness;
I cast bloody scraps to haul you in.
These hooves are un-ironed, and native
slice like rock into bone

as your head crowns in my hands,
its sodden pelt in salted waves
exposing the scalp — its shelf, well, pulse.

My Son The Horse

I dreamt my son had become a horse.
I was his red mother,
it showed in his hair and in his eye,
a fire leaping up inside.

He ran with me, tugging
at the training bit. His shoulder
was lining with new muscle,
his feathered foot cut the earth.

In his heart swelled a river.
He grew a hand daily
and the black of his father bloomed
a hide of dark roses.

In three years I will break him.
We will ride the high hill.
What power we will own
when his broad back strengthens.

Harvest

They have cut the corn
the colour of his hair.
The field lies exhausted with it, lovesick.

The sun lives now under his skin.
I warm myself by it,
and his womb-face when we wake to suckle.

Forgive me this, but his mouth
is the sweetest, ripest strawberry,
tempting, tempting,

and I cannot keep my hands
from the black furze
that hackles his salmon back.

One day it will darken, his hair,
to the nut brown of eyes
already reflecting rubies,

those eyes, birthed these nine months
from their milky husks,
ripened, like mine, from dark kernels.

Tooth Magic

For a week we watched it pearling
in the gum, intruded a finger
you defined your bony pain
on, whitening the head of a knuckle;

this, and the skin of my breast
razed in your mouth, you a flash
of retracted lips, teeth in black gums,
a blooded snout sly, laughing.

You surprise yourself
with your new found things,
your tooth a touchstone to quicken
fruit with in your hands.

You tap it on a cup, sound
its strength, plundering consonants
you pull out by the ears,
your sliced strings of sound miraculously healing.

KATE BINGHAM

Oxygen

Before you make a start there may be something else
you want to say, perhaps in a professional capacity

or just because it came up recently in a dream,
advertisement, or conversation and seems important.

This is the diminishing return you have to fight all afternoon
because a poem is like a rocket and the difficult bit

falls back to earth with a terrific crash which no one notices
for their ears are beating with drums and blood.

You press your nose to the window. Stones, tracks,
flowering cactus trees shrink into a khaki ocean

and the sea comes up from the horizon like a sunset backwards
as you carve a perfect turn away from the planet

and your bones go light. Unbuckle your belt
and fix yourself to the table now, you are writing effortlessly.

Pay no attention to the clock, the telephone,
the song of ambulances waiting for your imminent return,

and stay in orbit for as long as you have oxygen.
Say what it's like to be so far from home.

Things I learned at University

How to bike on cobblestones and where to signal right.
How to walk through doors held open by Old Etonians
and not scowl. How to make myself invisible in seminars
by staring at the table. How to tell Victorian Gothic
                                        from Medieval.
How to eat a Mars bar in the Bodleian. When to agree
with everything in theory. How to cultivate a taste for sherry.

Where to bike on the pavement after dark. How to sabotage
                                                   a hunt.
When to sunbathe topless in the Deer Park. When to punt.
How to hitch a lift and when to walk and where to run.
When not to address my tutors formally. How to laugh at
                                                   Latin puns
and when to keep quiet and preserve my integrity.
How to celebrate an essay crisis. When to sleep through
                                                   fire alarms.

How to bike no-handed, how to slip a condom on with one.
When to smoke a joint and when to swig champagne.
When to pool a tip and how to pull a pint. A bit of history.
When to listen to friends and whether to take them seriously.
At the same time how to scorn tradition and enjoy it.
How to live like a king, quite happily, in debt.

Two friends meet for lunch...

Two friends meet for lunch in The Royal Oak
in February. Oxford is ice. I'm nervous,
early. I avoid the barman's eye. Sip coke.

This is the afternoon I loved you first,
clenched throat uttering little carbonated hiccups
of surprise as the door's bell glittered.

Loved instantly your jacket and boots and lips
and hair. Your temperature. Thought: *this is it.*

You nod in my direction and lean at the bar.
Afterwards told me you'd had no idea I felt like that
and joked in bed about my sudden conversion.

Say there's nothing more to it than charisma
but people can never get enough of you. Even the barman,
counting out your change, is passionate.

Face to Face

My mother claims she could tell when I was ill,
even before I felt it — something unfamiliar in the smell
of my breath would jar, like a wrong note.

Animals scent fear and this can stimulate
the natural dominance of one species over another.
Mum could identify the fragrance of dishonesty,

half-truths, white lies. Now we communicate in other ways,
by post, long distance telephone, and this is how relationships
turn sour. Intuition fades, language takes over.

In Passing

I would like to be a woman in a poem.
Something by Milosz, perhaps, or Brodsky,
mentioned at the end of a stanza
almost casually —

the flare of a skirt, bright red,
suspended and still vanishing round the corner
of a certain derelict building
in the poet's home town.

A laugh with music in it — bells! —
that sounds like the laugh of somebody else
the poet once knew, when he was younger.
Ah, but she never came to America.

Lemon and jasmine. Menthol cigarettes.
I won't mind that the poet
only notices what he has already remembered,
that the poem only hints.

Reading it you wouldn't be able to say
exactly who he saw,
but only that it was a woman
who reminded you of me.

Beaujolais

Still drunk at midnight we find a small French restaurant,
demand to eat frogs' legs, snails and *tarte tatin*.
We order more wine, more cigarettes from the machine
and laugh too much. Sarah laughs quietly as well,
at something we're not meant to know about yet,
but there it is in her breasts, her cup of sugary camomile,
curled up fluttering in the hollow of her throat,
not quite asleep. Vinegar rings the red-check table-cloth,
there's ash in the cracks between the demerara cubes,
a Michaelmas daisy in a vase. We laugh and laugh
because it's Friday and everything seems hilarious
and suddenly this is what we should be frightened of.
The music finishes. Tomorrow comes. We cluster
at the foot of the stair and wait for taxis, for the thought of it
                                                    to pass.

6th December 1998

Your mouth is the start of a love affair
I have been planning ever since felt tip pen
disfigured my Goldilocks,

smudging the outline of her lips
and looping her cheek with forcep marks
which neither fairy liquid

nor two decades in the attic at home
can fade. Yours, my darling,
disappear in days.

In the delivery room I cry because you are so rare,
so beautiful all by yourself
it seems a tragedy to touch or kiss you,

even to let you live, slithering
towards ill-health and accident with every second,
every breath.

Meanwhile, you've opened your mouth
as wide as you can
and here I am holding you anyway,

feeling your bottom lip
curl under my salty nipple and your tongue contract
like a heart-beat.

How to Play

Think of a number — any — from one to forty-nine
and take away the common denominator of the dates
                                        of birth
of all your father's living relatives, including your own.
Divide by politics and religion and a piece of arable
with planning permission somewhere outside
                                        Northallerton,
round up to the nearest motorway junction
and subtract a fraction of the price you could have got.
Remainder everyone and everything you cared about
and halve your debt. Multiply the cost of living
where the jobs are by your quarterly telephone bill
and take away the square root of the bus route home,
the sum of last month's income tax and NI contributions.
Square the company's responsibility towards its
                                        shareholders,
factorial your hours. Calculate average one night stands
per annum as a function of loss to the power of love,
the difference between a round of drinks and the
                                        little black
stretchy number with the sweet-heart neck you wear
with nothing underneath but perfume and deodorant.
Multiply by fifty-two Saturdays a year and dance all night
to the tune of twenty-four million pounds. Divide by one.

OWEN SHEERS

Hedge Foal

At first we saw just the mare,
her swollen stomach deflated,
the wax on her teats broken,
standing, head low, by the hedge,
waiting for something to happen.

Then the afterbirth, discarded by her side:
a jelly fish placenta,
its bloody tentacles and loose, clear skin
slick over dock leaves and nettles.
The bitten umbilical cord like red steel rope.

And then finally, the foal,
cast deep in the hedge,
where it had rolled down the slope,
finding its all-hinge legs too collapsible
and its pulpy hooves too soft.

Suspended in blackthorn,
hung by bindatwine round its lips,
pulling them forward to a pucker.
Still and patient; an embryo
awaiting its birth back into the field.

Harvest

(for S.)

Sitting beneath the horse chestnut tree
we were surprised by a fall of conkers.
Miniature mines, through fathoms of leaves,
pelting our backs and our shoulders.
You began to gather them in,
squeezing out their secrets,

and those you picked you kept,
holding them tight to your stomach,
as if you had been stabbed, and were
bleeding conkers from the wound.
When they became too many,
you trusted me with some, which I held,
a bunch of knuckles in my fist.
But my sweat dulled their sheen,
turned them, dark liver brown to faded bay,
and when I gave them back to you,
you said it would always be this way;
because I am a man, and I have acid hands.

Learning the Language

Beneath the old oak in Llanddewi,
its tiny brains of mistletoe
showing in silhouette against the white sky;

this was where to find them.
Hard knots of hair and mucus
the paper twistings of a nervous hand,

packaged and pulled in the guts of an owl,
dropped with an upward swallow,
a single feathered heartbeat in the throat.

They translate in the warm water,
unfurl and loosen their fibres,
disclosing broken histories of bone;

a few lines of vertebrae, the clipping of a claw,
the greased and shrunken feather of a finch,
the miniature hinge of a shrew's jaw.

Laying out their patterns beneath the bright lamp,
I try to piece it together on the damp black paper —
arranging death sentences.

Stammerer on Scree

This slope is my language.
A shifting skin of stone
that slips under my grip,
feet peddling the one moving spot,
sharded slate, flowing hard water.

But when I am still,
crabbed against its steepness,
cheek to its side, a child on its mother,
then it stops.
Stone-ticks out to quiet,
rests itself on the mountain,
meaning everything.

Until I move again,
when it spreads under my hand,
slides from under my climbing feet,
like words from under a memory,
vowels from under a tongue.

Night Bus

The girl with glitter in her hair
falls to sleep for a second against a stranger's shoulder,
leaves her mark, star-dust on his collar.

Two women with a mission get on.
They sit next to the lost, the forgotten,
slip their pamphlets into half-curled hands.

She's falling again, her eyes flicking like a faulty screen,
dipping to darkness, sparking to light,
nodding her head in time to her own unconsciousness.

"Look to Jesus and he will save you,
he will show you the path to righteousness, the path to right.
Only he will show you the way."

Finally her head drops, the inky hammer to the paper,
the judge's gavel, falling as slow as only the guilty sees it fall;
but stranger, the young man in Wrangler, doesn't move.

Him and the driver, who counts them in, animals to the ark,
then shuts his doors, which hiss as they close,
a flat glass palm-off to the unsaved outside.

But then he moves his arm, a slow over-arm bowl,
over her resting head, then down across her shoulders,
a denim scarf of late night love, fingers stroking.

They're out of pamphlets, so the two women leave,
but others come to take their places,
sit and watch the scene behind their reflections,
                              the day's credits roll.

Except for Wrangler man, whose own head has dipped now
so he can smell the scent of her hair and kiss her there,
just lightly on the top of her head.

And isn't that what we want anyway?
For love to come to us in our sleep,
to come to us here and now, when we least expect it,
when we need it.

She sinks deeper into her sleep, and deeper into him,
while his eyes watch the closed lids of hers,
and he tries not to disturb her with his breathing.

For love to get on and sit next to us,
to bring a halt to this night bus, and its endless
                              midnight ellipsis
of stops and stops and stops....

Sea Reading

(for H.M.)

Thick skinned in wetsuits, sitting on surf boards,
we are learning to read again,
tracing, in the distance, the phrases of the waves.

Under the sun we watch each swell,
familiarise ourselves with their false promises,
the words that fail to make the page.

We wait, between the speech marks of distant gulls,
between the blank paper of the beach
and the last line of the horizon.

We wait for the sentence of water,
kamikazing itself towards the shore, that will allow us
                                        our fluency,
our moment of balance on the tightrope of the wave,

before it cuts us short, rubs us out
in a diaspora of white water,
leaving us to struggle back through our new language,

back to where, resting in a caesura,
showing only their heads, an ellipsis of seals
tells us it will continue,

but that for now the water is preparing its speech,
drawing upon its vocabulary of waves,
which are still just ideas, growing in the mind of the sea.

Stopped in the Street

It was your mouth which unlocked me
not the dark half-moons of dirt beneath your nails

or the street's cologne, which you wore,
rich and sweet with slept-in grime —

I've built a city side against such things,
used now, to keeping pain in the corner of my eye.

But your mouth, down and out in your face,
full with the pebble of absence, chewing on air,

stuck, the jaw repeating on a sound, scratched
somewhere in your head; I had to stop for that,

feeling once more the catch of consonants in the throat,
and the stubborn implosives, packed with potential behind
                                           clenched teeth.

And that is why, in the silence that you spoke,
I dropped those coins into your up-reached palm,

if for nothing else, to hear their chink,
their completed sound carried home, the simple sentence
                                           of money

which you busked from me without knowing,
singing as you did my secret signature tune so well.

KAREN GOODWIN

Wolf

First sight of the Pyrenees —
nothing but us and the car's spotlight
pushed out before us like a cold antennae.

Your hand at the wheel, gauged our way
through darkness, kept to the inside wall
of rock, our only compass from the edge.

Rain began to clip the roof, its thin pulse
thickened on windows, drummed its hooves
into a storm, drawing us in at each bend.

Suddenly, the sky lit up, white and feverish
the electric trees and the figure of a wolf
flashed across our path, made us swerve,

look back. I was terrified, an omen I was sure,
holding a great blank for our future,
the white heat of a sky doubled in its stomach.

That night, as I lay in your arms, I listened
for the howl of cold through your veins,
glimpsed the marble streak behind your eyes.

Ballet

Every Saturday, hair scraped and stabbed
with pins, temples throbbing
to the iron piano, ankles
bound in neat, pink silk,

the door opened on our bodies
to become less. Slighter than feathers,
transformed to a cat's step, papery hands
held, while the untrained breath

shuddered in our bones,
as if one birth were not enough.
We pushed and locked our hips,
grew tall with invisible string,

but time brought on breasts;
shadows on the mirrored walls.
And I foresaw a future of being less
in order to balance on my toes.

The Summerhouse

The house stands empty now —
cold and unvisited
as a February coast.

I dip under the lintel
which drags its piece of driftwood
over the door, creaks

as it always did, when opened
summers ago. Cobwebs blur
the edges of things;

shawls thick with flies,
that stare back at me
from their mummified deathloom,

brittle, drained of juice.
Only the window struggles
for a view against nettles,

the push of time in the grass;
my mother's voice still
scratching at the day's brightness

inside her hot, sealed jar.

Salome

Your name sparkles with promise,
a rosebud, a constellation,
a deep gorge running
through centuries of rock.

Salome; the slow bell tolls
through cities, fields throw
open their innocent skirts
and are ravaged by the wind.

And you, before uncle, mother,
God, dance naked, unashamed
as a child, leg swung wide —
practising for some older role.

In the future, your uncle's prize
lay waiting; the severed head
of St. John, his hair's damp
spaghetti for you to stroke.

Fallen Star

All that summer the roses
put out their thorns along our garden wall;
a bramble of wire that almost fizzled to touch it.

We were practising for gala gymnastics
on a rug of lawn, the grass flattening
under the weight of my body as I carried you
into the air on the arabesque of my feet.

As if the world paused in that moment,
the earth held sweet and damp under me,
a tangle of mowers digested in the distance,
your mouth torn open to the sky,

before my leg buckled,
and the roses caught you with hooked claw —
a comet's tail of blood burning on your thigh.

Brynhildr

A raven's wing severs her face
as she bends to work,
black hair on white features,
a shadow over the sun.

Each day the window
rehearses his return,
she stitches in its broad light,
beads of blood jewel her skin.

She no sooner belongs here
than a wolf on a farm,
fire crackles in the whites
of her eyes, a rasp of nettles

serves for her tongue.
She burns to get beyond
these walls, grow like gorse,
spiked and hostile to every touch.

The Sin-eaters

The night was an elderberry
darkening; veins collecting thunder,
roped from our huts
to the windlashed lanes —

time had forgotten us,
our children's cries sparkled like rain,
the suddenness of tapers
dwindled, became lost.

At the hill's summit
we knelt among the dead,
ate the rotten gifts from their chests;
flesh of berries, mouths and holes

of skin, until the sky
whitened its pearl at their jaws
and we were left among the earth's
scatterings; damaged fruit

the world's shame turns in our stomachs.

Ancient

As if entering the cold tomb
of her skull; honeycomb
sealed by salt sand, a desert of dust:

the room shrinks
to a pool of light, hovering above ground.
Along her skin, opalescent

as a paper lantern, veins welded
to her arm in hot metal inscription,
scant dress blunting the angle of bones.

She invites me to touch her —
one finger hooked, redoubled with string
drawing me in like breath or water —
marvelling how her body has beaten
the stars to heaven, outwitted
the moon's pale crucible, how later still

the curve of her arm will echo
my ancient own.

EMYR LEWIS

o Rhyddid

Hon yw dinas y pethau coll
'ddaliwyd yn y bwlch rhwng pnawn dydd Sul
a gweddill amser; pethau y bu stamp
eneidiau arnynt unwaith; nawr ar goll.

Mewn cwteri, o dan bontydd trên,
ym morderi'r parciau'n llechu'n saff
o afael atgof ac arwyddocâd,
ffotograffau pasport, menyg chwith,

poteli whisgi hanner-gwag o wlith,
allweddi cartref, arian mân; â'r baw,
sy'n lluwchio pan ddaw'r gwynt yn nyddiau'r cŵn,
yn bwrw arnynt am yn ail â'r glaw.

Heb eu claddu, heb eu marwnadu'n iawn:
nid oes defodau cymwys i bethau coll,
dim ond bytheirio byr o dro i dro
cyn ymryddhau, a'u gollwng nhw dros go'.

***

Yn yr amser amherffaith y caniateir
i ni freuddwydio ynddo, mewn seibiannau
rhwng ufuddhau i'r tician digyfaddawd,
pan fydd y sêr i'w gweld, a'r holl fydysawd
yn canu'i delynegion i ni'n dau,
yn nhywyllwch canhwyllau, yn sŵn ceir,
mae'r nos yn cau.

Am nad yw arad dychymyg yn troi'r stryd
yn fraenar cyfiaith lle cawn ni weddïo,
am nad yw'n codi'r trugareddau gollwyd
heb eu marwnadu'n iawn, am na all breuddwyd
drwsio egwyddor clociau, am y tro
yn salem ein noswylio, dyna glyd
yw byw dan glo.

from Freedom (Rhyddid)

This is the city of lost things, thrown away,
caught in the space between Sunday afternoon
and the rest of time; things that had the stamp
of souls upon them once; but not today.

In gutters, underneath the railway bridge,
and hiding in the borders in the park
safe from memory and significance
are passport photographs, a single shoe,

and whisky bottles now half-filled with dew,
and house keys, left-hand gloves, small change;
                              the grime
drifts over them when dog-day breezes blow,
and rain beats down on them in wintertime.

They've not been buried, not been elegised:
there are no rites for the discarded things,
you may just curse them briefly now and then,
then let them go, don't think of them again.

***

In the imperfect time when we have the right
to dream a little, in the occasional pause
between obeying the merciless ticking
when we can feel the whole universe singing
its lyrics to us when the stars are bright,
in candle darkness, in the sound of cars,
there comes the night.

The imagination cannot plough up the street
into a fallow place where we can pray,
it cannot pick up the lost discarded things
whose elegy was not sung, imaginings
can't change the way of clocks, and so today
in the salem of our evening, it's sweet
to hide away.

Yma mae ein cyfaddawd, ein hamser cain,
rhwng diniweidrwydd rhemp ein caru cyntaf
a'r llwch anadlwyd gennym ers blynyddoedd
yn llundain-ddoeth, yn gyfrwys fel dinasoedd.
Rhyngddynt, a rhwng y coed ar Lannau Taf
noswyliwn mewn dawns olaf yn sŵn brain,
ryw noson braf.

Mewn Eglwys

Disgleirio mae sêr
canhwyllau'r werin,
gwerth hatlin o wêr
i'r Forwyn Fair,
a phob un yn aberth,
yn weddi ddistaw,
yn gadw cyfrinach
heb dorri gair.

Cael seibiant mae saint
Cymdeithas yr Iesu
rhag synio am faint
dirgelion gras,
eu llygaid yn llarpio'r
goleuni glanwedd
a'u sibrwd yw *Sancta
simplicitas.*

Disgyn mae Duw
drwy grac yn y nenfwd
fel glöyn byw
at oleuni'r fflam,
er mwyn whare cwato
â'r llafnau disglair
a byw yn beryglus
heb wybod pam.

Here is our well-fashioned time, our compromise
between the wild innocence of first loving
and the dust that we have been breathing for years,
London-wise, sophisticated as cities.
Between the trees where the Taff is flowing
we rest a last dance to the night-birds' cries,
one fine evening.

(translation by Grahame Davies)

In a Church

Starlight-bright,
the people's tapers:
a tallow mite
for Mary mild,
each one a gift,
a silent praying,
keeping its secret
unbeguiled.

The saints of wood
lay down their burden
of bad and good,
mysterious grace.
Their eyes devour
this pure radiance,
whispering *Sancta
simplicitus.*

God flutters down
through a chink above them,
a moth that's drawn
to flame and light,
playing hide and seek
with a burning knife-edge,
courting danger
without knowing why.

(translation by Elin ap Hywel)

IWAN LLWYD

Iawn, gei di ofyn cwestiwn personol

"Sure you can ask me a personal question" — *Diane Burns*

S'mai?
   Na, dydw i ddim yn Wyddel.
Na, nid Llychlynwr.
   Na, dwi'n Gymro, yn Gymro Cymraeg.
Na, nid o'r Iseldiroedd.
   Na, nid o Cumbria.
Na, nid o Gernyw.
   Na, nid Sais.
Na, dydan ni ddim wedi darfod amdanom.
   Ia, Cymro
O?
   Felly dyna lle gest ti'r acen yna.
Dy hen hen nain, huh?
   Tywysoges Gymreig, huh?
Gwallt fel Nia Ben Aur?
   Tyd i mi ddyfalu. O Sir Fôn?
O, felly roedd gen ti ffrind oedd yn Gymro?
   Mor agos â hynny?
O, felly roedd gen ti gariad oedd yn Gymro?
   Mor dynn â hynny?
O, felly roedd gen ti forwyn oedd o Gymru?
   Cymaint â hynny?
Oedd, roedd hi'n ofnadwy be wnaethoch chi i ni.
   Rwyt ti'n garedig iawn yn ymddiheuro.
Na, wn i ddim lle gei di gawl cennin.
   Na, wn i ddim lle gei di frethyn Cymreig yn rhad fel baw.
Na, nid fi wnaeth hwn. Fe brynais i o yn Next.
   Diolch i ti, dwi'n licio dy wallt ti hefyd.
Dwn i ddim os oes rhywun yn gwybod ydi'r Edge yn Gymro
                       go iawn.
   Na, wnes i ddim cynganeddu cyn brecwast.
Na, fedra'i ddim canu cerdd dant.
   Na, dydw i ddim mewn côr meibion.
Wnes i rioed chwarae rygbi na gweithio mewn pwll glo.

Sure, you can ask me a personal question

"Sure you can ask me a personal question" – *Diane Burns*

How's it going?
   No, I'm not an Irishman.
No, not a Scandinavian.
   No, I'm a Welshman, a Welsh-speaking Welshman.
No, not from the Netherlands.
   No, not from Cumbria.
No, not from Cornwall.
   No, not an Englishman.
No, we're not extinct.
   Yes, a Welshman.
Oh?
   So that's where you got that accent.
Your great-great grandmother, huh?
   A Welsh princess, huh?
Hair like Nia Ben Aur?
   Let me guess. From Anglesey?
Oh, so you had a friend who was a Welshman?
   As close as that?
Oh, so you had a lover who was a Welshman?
   As tight as that?
Oh, so you had a maid who was from Wales?
   As much as that?
Yes, it was terrible what you did to us.
   It's very kind of you to apologise.
No, I don't know where you can get leek soup.
   No, I don't know where you can get Welsh cloth dirt cheap.
No, I didn't make this, I bought it in Next.
   Thank you, I like your hair as well.
No, I don't know if the Edge is a real Welshman.
   No, I didn't write *cynghanedd* before breakfast.
No, I can't sing *cerdd dant*.
   No, I'm not in a male voice choir.
I never played rugby or worked in a coal mine.
   Yeah, uh-huh, the muse.

Ia, Uh-huh, yr awen.
Uh-huh. Ia. Yr awen. Uh-huh. Y Fam
Ddaear. Ia. Uh-huh. Uh-huh. Yr awen.
Na, wnes i ddim gradd yng ngwaith Dylan Thomas.
Oes, mae 'na lawer ohonom ni yn yfed gormod.
Feder rhai ohonom ni ddim yfed digon.
Nid wyneb lleiafrifol mo hwn.
Fy wyneb i ydi o.

Dan Ddylanwad

Roedd diffyg ar yr haul
wrth hedfan môr Iwerydd.
Welwn i ddim mo'r golau i gyd,
ddim eto, nes cyrraedd glan,
dim ond gweld rhan o'r darlun,
rhan o'r pictiwr cyfan:

yn y cysgod, filoedd o droedfeddi oddi tana'i
dan haen o rew, dan oerni'r iâ,
gwlad yr addewid, yr Eden eitha,
ar lannau'r Iorddonen rydd a heini,
gwlad fabwysiedig Lennon a Hockney a Brecht,
gwlad y ffoadur a'r pechadur a'r pur
o galon, y brodorion a'r Brodyr,
gwlad gorthrwm a chwlwm a chwalfa,
gwlad fu'n gaethglud a Gwladfa...

Amtrak, playback, Burgerbars a Big-Mac
Freeway boardwalk, Broadway Don't Walk
Greyhound southbound, New Jersey Turnpike
Golden Gate Interstate, Bourbon Street first-strike:

gwlad o enwau sy'n fwy cyfarwydd erbyn hyn
nag enwau Palesteina neu Rodd Mam: —
Boston a'r Little Big Horn, Alberquerque a Santa Fe,
Elvis frenin, Martin Luther King a JFK
'stuck inside of Mobile with the Memphis blues again'
a thaith drwy Dallas â'n hwyach wrth dyfu'n hen:

108

Uh-huh, Yeah. The muse. Uh-huh. Mother
          Earth. Yeah. Uh-huh. Uh-huh. The muse.
No, I didn't do a degree in the works of Dylan Thomas.
          Yes, some of us do drink too much.
Some of us can't drink enough.
          This isn't a minority face.
It's my face.

(translation by Grahame Davies)

Under the Influence

There was an eclipse
as we flew the Atlantic.
We won't see all the light,
not yet, until we reach land,
only see a part of the picture,
part of the whole scene:

in the shadow, thousands of feet below
under a layer of ice, under the frost's coldness,
the promised land, uttermost Eden,
on the banks of the free young Jordan,
adopted land of Hockney, Brecht and Lennon,
the land of the refugee, the sinner and the pure
of heart, of the natives, of the Brothers,
the land of oppression and attachments and separation,
the land that was captivity and colony....

          Amtrak, playback, burgerbars and Big-Mac
          Freeway, boardwalk, Broadway Don't Walk
          Greyhound, southbound, New Jersey Turnpike
          Golden Gate Interstate, Bourbon Street first-strike:

a land of names that by now are more familiar
than the names of Palestine or Mother's Gift —
Boston and the Little Big Horn, Alberquerque and Santa Fe,
Elvis the king, Martin Luther King and JFK
"stuck inside of Mobile with the Memphis blues again"
and the journey through Dallas that gets longer as you
                                        get older:

gwlad Hendrix a Janis a John Lee Hooker,
a Blue Suede Shoes a Return to Sender,
gwlad o golofnau mwg a siwrneiau maith,
o farchog yn diflannu drwy lwch y machlud ym mhen
                                                    pella'r paith:

    Flat-top backdrop, gwylia rhag y speed-cop,
    Slo-mo, coffee to go, all-nite Miller Lite
    Automatic Instamatic pig-roast West coast
    Gateway Safeway Bala Cynwyd Parkway:

gwlad cyfle a Chaliffornia a strydoedd Philadelphia,
o Dduw'r teledu a Holywood a haleliwia,
gwlad Bob Dylan a Dylan Thomas, gwlad alltud y bardd,
gwlad Goronwy a Madog a llwyth o frodorion hardd
sy'n wyn fel Gwalia, yn odli'n Gymraeg, gwlad ifanc
sy'n dal i dyfu, i genhedlu, i ddwyn y nyth bob cyfyl
a gwthio'r hen gywion yn ddiseremoni dros yr ymyl:
gwlad y saint a'r hwrod hy, y Cosa Nostra a'r Crist seliwloid
y blŵs ac mae hi'n bleser, yr hipi trist a'r hapusrwydd
                                                    paranoid:

Roedd diffyg ar yr haul
wrth groesi'r arfordir i'r gogledd o Bangor, Maine,
o Fangor i Fangor,
o'r hen fyd i'r byd newydd
yn breuddwydio am yrru
mewn Mustang soft-top ar Highway 61.

the land of Hendrix and Janis and John Lee Hooker,
and Blue Suede Shoes and Return to Sender,
the land of the pillar of fire and the long journeys,
of the rider disappearing through the sunset dust at the rim of
the prairie:

Flat-top backdrop, look out for the speed-cop,
Slo-mo, coffee to go, all-nite Miller Lite
Automatic Instamatic pig-roast West coast
Gateway Safeway Bala Cynwyd Parkway:

the land of opportunity and California and the streets of
Philadelphia,
of the television God and Hollywood and hallelujah,
the land of Bob Dylan and Dylan Thomas, the land of the
poet's exile,
the land of Goronwy and Madog and a tribe of handsome
natives
as white as Wales, rhyming in Welsh, a young land
still growing, generating, taking over the nest at every chance
and shoving the older chicks unceremoniously over the edge:
the land of the saints and the bold whores, the Cosa Nostra
and the celluloid Christ,
of the Blues and it's a pleasure, of the sad hippy and
the paranoid happiness:

There was an eclipse
as we crossed the coast to the north of Bangor, Maine,
from Bangor to Bangor,
from the old world to the new world,
dreaming about driving
in a soft-top Mustang along Highway 61.

(translation by Grahame Davies)

GWYNETH LEWIS

Rhodd

"Oriawr yn anrheg? Amser gan fy ngŵr?
Sut allet ti roi breichled aur yn glwyf

mor ddwfn am fy ngarddwrn? Y mae troi
y rhod ddyfeisgar ym mherfeddion hon

yn elyn inni, mae fel ffiws ar fom
a fydd yn chwythu pob cariad rhyngom

yn deilchion ryw ddydd. Na, nid heddi chwaith,
ond er mor gywrain ydyw'r gwaith

ar ddannedd yr olwynion, mae eu taith
yn llyncu'n bywyd, yn ei rwygo'n rhacs

i ebargofiant." "Amser *yw* fy rhodd
i ti. Nid ei beirianwaith — y mae'n anodd

gweld gwallt yn gwynnu — ond ei led
a'i ddyfnder, serch â'i gysgodion caled

a'r gwybod am angau. Na, mae cariad dau
fel coelcerth a daw'r eiliadau

ato yn wyfynnod brau
mewn heidiau i edmygu'r golau

cyn i ni farw. Ond, am y tro,
gwisg dy oriawr aur fel O

a chofia ein bod yn gylch, ac yn ei ganol
y gwacter ffrwythlon a fydd ar ein hôl."

Gift

"A watch as a gift? Time from my husband?
How could you give me a gold bracelet that will wound

my wrist so deeply? After all,
the devious wheel in these entrails will

turn into our enemy, be the fuse
on a bomb that blows all love between us

into smithereens some day. No, not
today, but the sharp teeth of the clock

are so precise that their journeying
will chew our lives up, tearing

our shreds to nothingness." "Time *is* my gift
to you. Not its mechanics —

it's bitter to see the hair turn white — but its breadth
and depth, romantic love with its hard shadows

and consciousness of death.
No, married love's a blaze

and the seconds swarm to it
like frail moths, drawn to admire the light

before we die. But, for now, let it go —
wear your gold watch like an O

to remind you we're a wheel and at its hub's
the fertile void that will come after us."

Adroddiad y Patholegydd

Y Ffeithiau

Disgrifiad
Benyw, pum troedfedd, mewn gwth o oed.
Digon iach, serch hynny. Ei dannedd ei hun.

Briwiau
Bu mewn damwain, fel pe bai criw
wedi ei damsgen yn wyllt o dan draed.
Mwd yn y clwyfau, sy'n ddu gan laid.

Roedd ei gwaed yn wenwynig:
olion mogadon a digitalis.
Dim digon i ladd
ond byddai'n ddifywyd,
ac yn teimlo fel claf.

Trywaniad â chyllell. Ond nid digon dwfn
i fod yn angheuol. Mae'r diffyg gwaed
yn awgrymu mai trawma ar gelain oedd hwn.

Dadansoddiad
Dioddefodd y gwrthrych o leiaf dair
ffordd o drengi. Fel arfer mae dwy
yn ddigon i berswadio corff
i aros yn farw. Anodd coelio nerth
ewyllys hon a'r hunan-werth
a'i cadwodd yn fyw. Sut mae lladd iaith?
A oes ganddi gorff
a all garu, cenhedlu, dewis peidio â bod?

QED
Fy nghasgliad, Carma, yw fod y dystiolaeth
yn amwys. Dewiswch chi'r achos.
Amgaeaf, fel arfer, y dystysgrif marwolaeth.

114

Pathology Report

The Facts

Description
Female, five foot, extremely old.
Quite healthy, though. Has kept her teeth.

Injuries
Had met with an accident, as if she'd been
trampled underfoot by a mob.
Mud in the wounds, which are black with dirt.

Her blood was toxic:
traces of mogadon and digitalis.
Not enough to kill
but she'd be listless
and feeling ill.

A knife-wound. But not deep enough
to be fatal. The lack of blood
suggests a trauma on a corpse.

Analysis
The subject suffered at least three
ways of dying. Two are normally
sufficient to persuade a body
to stay dead. It's hard to credit the strength
of this one's will and the self-belief
that kept her alive. How does one kill
a language? Does she have a body
that can love, have children, choose not to be?

QED
My conclusion, Karma, is that the evidence
is ambiguous. You choose the cause.
I enclose, as usual, the death certificate.

(translations by Richard Poole, with the author)

115

IFOR AP GLYN

Tri Darlleniad Trychinebus Ynys Prydain

Rhif 1: Caerdydd 1989

Chapter 1989
Canolfan Celfyddydau
ym mhrifddinas Cymru;
a darganfûm fy mod
yn rhan o 'noson *ryng*-wladol'
yn fy ngwlad fy hun,
yn rhannu'r *right-on* gymeradwyaeth
hefo rhyw Romanian o fardd
o Lundan;
Bogdan ap Glyn, neu rwbath....

Ro'n i felly'n un o'r egsotica
ac roedd 'na gling-ffilm
rhyngof i a'r gynulleidfa,
naill ai i 'nghadw inna'n ffres
neu i gadw ogla'r Gymraeg
rhag lledu trwy weddill y ffrij....

Roedd o fel mynd i'r ardd gefn
a ffendio llond bws o dwristiaid
yn codi dy datws fel swfenîrs

– *Y'all wanna talk some Welsh at us here bo'?*
– *Play us some rug-bee!*
– *Show us yore teeth!*
– *Say! Ken y'all juggle with* **fahve** *pieces of bayra breeth?*
– *Show us how y'all make them thar* **traditional** *shawls
  outa chicken wool!*
– *Shee-it! Ah didn' even know chickens* **had** *wool!*
– *Sgynnon nhw ddim*
– *What you say bo'?*
– *They haven't any*
– *Thelma! Git back on the bus!!*

116

The Three Disastrous Poetry Readings
of the Island of Britain

No. 1: Cardiff 1989

Chapter 1989,
an arts centre
in Wales' capital city,
and I discovered that I was
part of an *inter*-national evening,
one of the 'other' cultures
and in my own country,
sharing the *right-on* clapping and cheering
with some Romanian bard from London,
Bogdan ap Glyn or something....

And so I was part of an exotic experience
which put cling film between me and the audience,
either to keep me fresh
or to stop the smell of Welsh
from tainting the rest of the fridge....

It was like going into your back garden
and finding a bus-load of tourists
digging up your spuds for souvenirs

  — *Y'all wanna talk some Welsh at us here bo'?*
  — *Play us some rug-bee!*
  — *Show us yore teeth!*
  — *Say! Can y'all juggle with **fahve** pieces of bayra breeth?*
  — *Show us how y'all make them thar **traditional** shawls
    outa chicken wool!*
  — *Shee-it! Ah didn' even know chickens **had** wool!*
  — *Sgynnon nhw ddim*
  — *What you say bo'?*
  — *They haven't any*
  — *Thelma! Git back on the bus!!*

Ond 'nôl yn Chapter 'ro'n i'n wynebu cynulleidfa
oedd yn Gymry (gan eu bod i gyd yn byw yma)
oedd yn gweld pob diwylliant fel picnic fyrdda
er byth yn ystyried mynd atynt i fyta,
(ond diawl! maen nhw'n betha handi anghyffredin
i'r rhain, fatha gwartheg,
grafu'u tina yn eu herbyn....)

Rhyngwladol Schmyngwladol,
mae'r Gymraeg jest yn *normal*....

o Golau yn y Gwyll
Clirio'r tŷ mewn cwmwl tystion

(Elfyn: Llanrwst)
Lladd ystyr mae marw iaith,
nid diffodd golau ond sathru'r bylb,
nid chwythu'r gannwyll ond porthi'r moch â'r gwêr.
Heddiw roedd hi
yn oslef gain ac islais main,
and then....
it's just not there.

Amhosib fydd ail-greu iaith o'r bag bún du
llawn treigliadau anghynnes
mor ddiwerth â dannedd gosod ail-law,
y tronsiau o frawddegau,
botymau sbâr o enwau
a'r berfau a wiwerwyd
at achlysur na ddaw.

Y Saesneg biau'r stryd erbyn hyn,
a chadair fy nhad yn wag
wedi methu ag atal y lli.

Ond baich ardal arall, ers tro byd,
sydd yn hawlio fy nghalon i:

118

But back in Chapter
I was facing an audience,
a Welsh one, an' all, by virtue of residence
who saw other cultures like picnic tables
though eating from them was not one of their foibles,
but hell! They're so handy, whether laden or unladen,
for this lot, like cattle, to scratch their arses against them....

so... International, Schminternational,
Welsh is just *normal*....

from Light in the Darkness
Clearing the house in a cloud of witnesses

(Elfyn: Llanrwst)

The death of language murders meaning,
not the switching of a light, but the crushing of the bulb,
not the blowing of a candle, but feeding its tallow to swine.
Today it was alive and more;
its undertones acute
its timbre refined
et puis...
ça n'est pas là encore.

...It's impossible to recreate a language
from the black binbag full of distasteful mutations
(as worthless as second hand teeth in pawn)
the sentences like long johns,
nouns like spare buttons
and those verbs squirreled away
for a day that did not dawn...

... English has domain in our street now
and my father's chair is empty
having failed to turn back the waves...

but another place's burden, for some time now,
has had *my* heart enslaved

nhw yw fy nheulu yn awr,
Cheryl a Dave, Julie a Wayne;
nhw yw'r dyfodol; nhw yw fy ngwaith;
lladd ystyr mae marw iaith.

I've always wished I could speak Welsh

(Wayne: Abertridwr)

Mae'r dyfodol yn ddyn hoffus o amheus
ar sesiwn pnawn, yn gwenu fel gwn,
yn chwerthin fel *exocet,*

yn gwmnïwr da, fel yr heulwen a ddaw
trwy ffenestri'r pnawn, yn dân yn dy gwrw
ac yn ddawns ar dy dafod.

Ond er bod y pnawn yn llachar o beintiau
a'r nos bell yn llawn posibiliadau,
dyn peryg yw'r dyfodol,

yn diflannu i'r gwyll heb godi'i rownd
yn d'adael chwap yn anterth y mwg
yn wynebu'r presennol prin,

am un ar ddeg, heb ddim
ond 'y *kudos* o fod yn bocedwag'
yn heiroglyff ar gefn mat cwrw

a anghofir gennyt ar y bar,
wrth faglu trwy'r drws.
Mae'n dechrau bwrw....

they are my family now,
Cheryl and Dave, Julie and Wayne,
they are the future, they are my calling
the death of a language murders meaning.

I've always wished I could speak Welsh

(Wayne: Abertridwr)

The future's a likeably dodgy bloke
on an afternoon 'sesh', smiling like a gun
and laughing like an exocet,

he's good company, like the sunshine that flies
through the afternoon's windows, firing up your beer
and dancing on your tongue.

But although the afternoon is bright with pints
and the night long distant, replete with possibilities,
the future's a dangerous man,

disappearing into the night without buying his round,
leaving you at eleven as the fug is at its thickest,
face to face with your vanishing present,

leaving you nothing
but the "kudos of having been kidded"
a *bon mot* hieroglyphed on a beer mat's back

which you forget, on the bar,
as you stumble through the door,
as it begins to pour....

Croesi'r Bont

(Dave: Tremorfa)

Digwyddodd heddiw,
p'nawn 'ma yn y *pressing plant*,
hefo'r hogan o Lanelli
sy'n holi hynt fy ngwersi,

digwyddodd rhywbeth sbesial
sydd fel cyri yn cyrraedd,
yn droli ac yn drimins
ac yn lliain wen i gyd;

deallais sbeis ei geiriau,
eu profi am y tro cynta,
cyd-fwydo yn gariadus
o un ddesgil yn lle dwy;

digwyddodd heddiw,
a thân gwyllt y Gymraeg
yn goleuo'r nos, yn gwreichioni pob sgwrs
wrth gerdded o'r dafarn yn ôl i'w thŷ.

Crossing Over

(Dave: Tremorfa)

It happened today,
this afternoon in the pressing plant
with the girl from Llanelli
who asks how my lessons are going.

Something special happened,
like the arrival of a biriani,
all trolley and trimmings
and starched white tablecloth;

I understood the spice in her speech,
tasted it for the first time,
as we lovingly co-spooned
from one dish instead of two;

it happened today,
and a linguistic firework display
lit up the night,
scintillating our discussion
as we walked back from the pub
to her house.

(translations by the author)

TWM MORYS

Sefyll 'Rown

Sefyll rown ar fryn yn Arberth,
Ar fy nghefn roedd cwrwgl anferth,
Yn fy nhin yr oedd cenhinen,
A thelyn am fy ngwddw'n hongian.

Roedd fy ngwallt yn ymgordeddu,
Yn fy nhrwyn yr oedd llwy garu,
Am fy mhen roedd het fawr ddu,
Ac roedd fy llais yn ddyfn a chry'.

Cenais yr Eos a'r Glân Hedydd,
A'r Deryn Du sy'n Rhodio'r Gwledydd,
Pry Bach Bach, a'r Hen Ferchetan
Oll dan ddawnsio dawns y glocsan.

Ac wele'n ara' deg o'r dyfnjwn,
Ac i fyny i'r bryn lle'r oeddwn,
Hen hen hen ŵr efo ffon,
A meddai hwn: *You Spanish, John?*

Y Teithiwr

Doedd gen i ddim cyfoeth, dwi'n gaddo i chi,
ond deryn mewn cawell, a 'nghyllell a 'nghi.
Bob dydd byddai'r deryn yn canu'r un gân
a'r ci bach yn dawnsio o gwmpas y tân.
Ac mi godwn o'r gadair i gydio'n fy sach
i roi chwaneg o fin ar yr hen gyllell fach.

A dyma fi'n disgwyl, a'r llafn yn fy llaw,
a'r sach am fy sgwyddau yn mochel y glaw.
O ochor bryn uchel mi sbïais i cyd
nes y gwelwn y bont 'rochor arall i'r byd.
Ôn i'n disgwyl y teithiwr sy'n drewi o bres,
ac sy'n tincial fel clychau wrth ddŵad yn nes.

Welsh Airs

I was standing on a hill in Narberth,
A dirty great coracle on my back,
A leek in my bum,
A harp hanging round my neck.

My hair was interlaced,
There was a love-spoon through my nose,
On my head was a big black hat,
And my voice was deep and strong.

I sang the Nightingale and the Lark,
The Blackbird Who Wandered the World,
The Tiny Fly, and the Old Maid,
All the while doing the clog dance.

And very slowly from the abyss,
Up to the hill where I stood,
Came an old, old, old man with a stick,
And he said: *You Spanish, John?*

The Traveller

I had no wealth, believe me,
But a caged bird and a knife and a dog.
Every day the bird would sing the same song,
And the dog would dance around the fire.
And I'd get up from the chair to seize my sack,
To sharpen up the little knife again.

And so I waited with the blade in my hand,
And sack around my shoulders against the rain.
And from the side of a high hill I looked out so long
That I saw the bridge on the other side of the world.
I was waiting for the traveller who reeks of money,
And who tinkles like bells as he approaches.

Ac mi welwn o'r diwedd ddyn diarth yn dod,
yn cerdded fel 'tae 'na ddim pellter yn bod.
A chlywn i mo'r clychau, ond mi wyddwn i'n iawn
ar ei wyneb a'i wisg, fod ei goffrau o'n llawn;
"yn rhwydi y rhedyn, mi dalia'i o'n dynn,
ac mi drawa'i fy nghyllell i yn ei groen gwyn."

Ond pan ddaeth o'n agos a sefyll o 'mlaen,
mi glywais fy nghalon yn gollwng fel tsiaen,
ac mi gollais y gyllell yng nghanol y drain —
Yn y man lle disgynnodd, mi dyrrodd y brain.
Ac mi es efo'r teithiwr, oedd yntau â'i fryd
ar gael cyrraedd y bont 'rochor arall i'r byd.

Mi Gan' Nhw Ddisgwyl

Mi gan' nhw ddisgwyl nes plygu pebyll yr ŵyl,
Achos mae'u llofnod heb ddim awdurdod
Rhwng bod y dail yn dod a'r plant yn gwneud cychod,
A rhwng bod y cychod ar afon, a'u bod nhw wedi'u bachu,
Rhwng y chwedl a'r chwerthin, ac Ebrill a hanner Mehefin,
Rhwng dwi'n dy garu di, a chawod oer y conffeti,
Rhwng bwrdd llong y freuddwyd, a'r ddesg yn y swyddfa
                                                lwyd,
Rhwng bod y wlad yn rhydd, a'r iaith yn mynd i'w gilydd,
Rhwng y wledd a'r angladdau, rhwng agor ein llygaid a'u cau,
Rhwng ein bod ni'n gweld y ddôr, ac yn codi i'w hagor.

At last I saw a stranger coming,
Walking as if there were no such thing as distance.
I couldn't hear the bells, but I knew very well
By his face and his clothes that his coffers were full.
In the bracken nets I'll hold him fast,
And I'll put my knife in his white skin.

But when he came near, and stood before me,
I felt my heart give way like a chain.
And I lost the knife in the midst of the thorntrees;
The crows gathered in the place where it fell.
And I went with the traveller, who'd set his mind too
On reaching the bridge on the other side of the world.

They'll Have to Wait

They'll have to wait till the tents are folded.
Their signature has no authority here
Between the leaves coming and the children making boats;
Between the boats being on a river, and their being
                                on the ocean;
Between the berries being black, and their being snatched;
Between the story and the laughter, and April and half of June;
Between I love you and the cold shower of confetti;
Between the ship's bridge in the dream and the office desk;
Between the country flying open and the language folding up;
Between the feast and the funerals, opening our eyes
                                and closing them;
Between seeing the door and getting up to open it.

(translations by the author)

ELIN AP HYWEL

Deall Goleuni

(er cof am Gwen John)

Weithiau, ar b'nawniau Sul, a'r golau'n oer
mae hi'n gweld ei hwyneb am yr hyn ydi o —
a'r haul yn ysgythru esgyrn ei chernau,
a chylchoedd y blynyddoedd dan ei llygaid.

Ben bore, yn yr offeren
a'r lleill wrth eu pader mewn byd sy'n llawn goleuni —
syllai ar y plygion
yng ngwempl y lleian o'i blaen.
Sut all lliain gwyn fod unlliw â lluwch?

Neithiwr, wrth wawl y lamp, gosododd
dorth o fara a chyllell ar y bwrdd,
a chyn bwyta, codi ei phensel.

Heno, bydd hi'n gorffen y braslun,
yn tynnu llun y gath a'r gadair simsan. Gŵyr
y bydd gwallt y ferch sy'n plygu tua'r golau
yr un lliw â diferyn o waed sydd newydd sychu.

Duwiesau

Duwiesau Cymru —
duwiesau'r banadl, y deri, blodau'r erwain
yr esgyrn sychion, ewinedd yn y blew

— nid y chi oedd yn camu trwy 'mreuddwydion
flynyddoedd yn ôl yn fy ngwely hogan-ysgol

ond mân-dduwiesau llyweth y mynd a'r dod
a gwafrai'n anwadal drwy chwedlau Rhufain a Groeg,
yn enfys am eiliad, ac yna yn nant neu'n llwyn
wastad rhwng dau feddwl a dwy ffurf,

Understanding Light

(in memory of Gwen John)

Sometimes
on Sunday afternoons
in north light
she sees her face for what it really is —
a cold sun etches a cheekbone,
figuring the years' circles under her eyes.

At mass this morning
others at prayer in a world of light —
she stares at the folds
in coif and wimple.
How can linen be the colour of ash?

Last night, by lamplight, she placed
a loaf of bread, a knife, on the table
and before eating picked up her pencil.

Tonight she will finish the sketch.
She will draw the cat, the rickety chair.
She knows the girl's head against the light
will be
the colour of a drop of blood,
drying.

Goddesses

Goddesses of the Celts —
goddesses of broom, and meadowsweet and oakflower,
dry, rattling bones, claws buried deep in fur —

you weren't the ones who wobbled,
years ago, through my dreaming schoolgirl head.

I worshipped the little sprites, the come-day, go-day
quavering through the myths of Greece and Rome,

yn plesio rhyw ddyn, yn cuddio rhag rhyw dduw
yn newid eu henwau a'u hunain fel newid lipstic
Echo, Eos, Psyche, — merched chweched-dosbarth
yn chwerthin tu ôl i'w gwalltiau newydd-eu-golchi.

Dod i ddeall eich ffyrdd wnes i
yn araf, anfodlon, yn gyndyn fel boddi cathod
gyda phob clais a welais, pob cusan wag
pob modrwy yng nghledr llaw, dod i ddeall dicter —
sawru y gwaed ar y dwylo a gwres y tŷ haearn
clywed penglogau plant yn glonc yn y gwynt.

Freninesau y gwyllt, y lloerig, y pobl o'u coeau
y distawrwydd anghynnes, yr anesmwythyd mawr
— ry'ch chi'n cadw cwmni heno yn nâd y newyddion,
yn stelcio drwy'r stafell yn eich gynau sidan carpiog.
Mae blinder y blynyddoedd yn friw dan eich llygaid
a'ch crwyn yn afalau crychion:

ond mae'r fellten a'r daran yn drydan yng nghwmwl eich
                                                gwalltiau,
barclodiad rhyw gawres yn gengl o amgylch eich boliau
a meillion eich dicter gwyn yn dynn wrth eich sodlau.

Ynysoedd gwŷr cedyrn sy'n dymchwel wrth odre
                                                eich peisiau.

Cawl

Nid cerdd am gawl yw hon —
nid cerdd am ei sawr, ei flas na'i liw,
na'r sêr o fraster yn gusanau poeth
ar dafod sy'n awchu eu hysu

Nid cerdd am gawl yw hon,
am frathiad o foron tyner,
am sudd yn sugnad safri, hallt
na'r persli'n gonffeti o grychau gwyrdd

130

a rainbow one minute, the next a spring or tree,
wavering between two minds, two bodily forms,
trying to please some man, hide from some god,
changing their names, their selves, like choosing lipstick.
Echo, Eros, Psyche — sixth form nymphettes,
giggling behind their freshly shampooed hair.

I came to our goddesses slowly,
reluctant and painful, stubborn like drowning kittens.
With every bruise I've seen, each empty kiss,
each fallen ring, become apprentice Fury —
smelt the blood on your hands, the heat of the iron,
heard the skulls of children knocking on wind.

Goddesses of wild, mad, grief-stricken people,
of enormous silence, of terrible, unsaid things —
you're here tonight in the thin sound of the news,
stalking the room in your ragged silken gowns,
bone-weariness a bruise under shadowed eyes,
your skin crabbed like old apples —

yet lightning and thunder sing through your clouded hair,
your aprons gigantic knots around sagging bellies,
white clovers of anger still bloom in the print of your shoes.
In the sweep of your petticoats kingdoms crash and
                                              are gone.

Soup

This is not a poem about soup —
not the colour of soup, its smell, its taste
nor its stars of fat — searing kisses
on a tongue just aching to burn —

this is not a poem about soup,
the delicate bite of carrots,
the savoury, salt suck of liquid,
the parsley like crumpled green confetti.

Dim ond cawl oedd e wedi'r cyfan
— tatws a halen a chig a dŵr —
nid gazpacho na chowder na bouillbaisse,
bisque na velouté neu vichysoisse

Nid cerdd am gawl yw hon
ond cerdd am rywbeth oedd ar hanner ei ddysgu—
pinsaid o rywbeth fan hyn a fan draw,
mymryn yn fwy neu'n llai o'r llall
— y ddysgl iawn, llwy bren ddigon hir —
pob berwad yn gyfle o'r newydd
i hudo cyfrinach athrylith cawl.

Nid cerdd am gawl yw hon o gwbl
— nid cerdd am gawl, nac am ddiffyg cawl:
dim oll i'w wneud â goleuni a gwres
y radio'n canu mewn cegin gynnes
a lle wrth y bwrdd

Defnyddiol

Ys gwn i beth ddigwyddodd i hen fenywod fy
                              mhlentyndod?
Eu hetiau ffwr, eu llyfrau emynau parod,
a'u cariad yn wasgfa boeth
o frethyn cras a broitsys pigog?

Gwingwn a llithrwn o'u gafael
â chusan y froits yn glais ar fy moch.
Y tu ôl i'w ffws a'u hanifeiliaid marw
roedd hoglau tristwch yn biso sur.

"Cariad yw cariad," dwrdiai fy mam,
"Beth bynnag fo'i hoglau,
waeth pa mor bigog,"

132

After all, it was only soup,
— potatoes and meat and water and salt —
not gazpacho nor chowder nor bouillbaisse,
bisque or velouté or vichysoisse.

This is not a poem about soup,
but a poem about a thing half-learnt:
a pinch of something here and there
a soupçon more of this or that
— the one right bowl, a long enough spoon —
each boiling another chance
to witch the secret genius of soup.

This is not a poem, at all, about soup —
not a poem about soup, or the lack of soup;
nothing to do with heat and light,
the radio humming in a warm kitchen,
a place at the table.

Really Useful

What happened to the chapel ladies of childhood?
The fur hats, the ever-ready hymn books,
and their love, a hot squeeze
of rough tweed and spiky brooches?

I squirmed away from their hugs,
brooch-spikes a flowering bruise on my cheek.
Behind their fuss, their dead animals,
the smell of their sadness was sour like piss.

"Love is love," scolded my mother,
"whatever it smells like,
however spiky."

Ers hynny, cerais
a chefais fy ngharu —
cariad cysurus, weithiau,
yn llac a chynnes fel hen gordwroi;
cariad arall fel llenni net
sy'n dangos mwy nag a guddiant;
un cariad fel brathiad rhaff
a ysai ac a losgai fy nghnawd.

Dyma'r cariad a garwn:
cariad sydd fel cynfasau
o liain Iwerddon, gant y cant
eu gwead yn llyfn a chryf
heb oglau arnynt ond glendid a phowdwr:
cynfasau â digon o afael a rhuddin,
cynfasau na fydd yn ildio pwyth
pan glymaf nhw'n rhaff hir gwyn at ei gilydd,
eu taflu o'r ffenest, a diflannu i'r nos.

Since then, I've loved.
I've been loved.
An easy love at times,
saggy and baggy like old corduroy;
other loves like net curtains
showing more than they were trying to hide.
One love was a biting rope,
it burnt and ate my flesh.

This is the kind of love I'd like:
a love like bedsheets,
Irish linen, one hundred percent,
smooth textured, strong,
smelling of nothing but fresh air and powder:
sheets with backbone,
that don't yield a stitch
when I tie them together, a long white rope,
shimmy down through the window, make off in the night.

(translations by the author)

MEIRION MACINTYRE HUWS

Côt

Os ydwyf yn drwsiadus
a gwawr o wên i mi'n grys
fe hiraethaf am frethyn
fy nghôt dlotaf harddaf un.
Y gôt fu'n gyfaill gyhyd,
o oglau'r dafarn fyglyd
i sidan y gusan gudd,
o'r wên i'r goflaid drennydd,
o'r rhedyn i'r briodas,
yn dŷ, yn wely, yn was.
Y gôt fu'n gweiddi "I'r gad",
yn Brifwyl ac yn brofiad,
yn wead o'r ddafad ddu
yn hen, ond uwchlaw hynny
yn seintwar i ddau gariad
rhag tywydd lonydd y wlad.
Ei dwyn oedd dwyn hanes dau,
a'i dwyn oedd fy nwyn innau.

Lle mae cychod y tlodion

Lle mae'r tarmac yn graciau,
a sŵn cwch fel drws yn cau
yn rhywle, lle mae'r wylan
fudur â chur yn ei chân
wastad, a'r tai yn ddistaw,
ac oglau hallt ar y glaw,
lle mae'r gaeaf yn trafod
fy hynt a'r hyn sydd i fod.

Coat

I may wear a dawning smile for shirt,
my grooming you may note,
but still I long for the touch of the cloth
of my poorest greatest coat.

The coat that smelled of tavern-smoke,
that stayed my friend through much,
that felt the silk of a secret kiss
from smile to morning touch.

From mountain-side to marriage,
a servant, house and bed,
the coat that cried "To battle",
experienced, well-read.

They wove it from a black sheep's wool,
and threadbare as may be,
when autumn winds turned colder,
it gave us sanctuary.
And he who took it took our past
and stealing it, stole me.

The Boats of the Poor

Where the tarmac is cracked
and the sound of a boat is like a creaking door
somewhere, where the dirty
seagull always has pain in its song
where all the houses are silent,
where there's a salt smell to the rain,
where the winter discusses my business
and what may come tomorrow.

Lle mae cychod y tlodion
yn dweud eu dweud wrth y don
a dwy awr rhyngof a'r dydd,
dwyawr a hithau'n dywydd,
mae'n flêr, a does 'run seren
heno i mi uwch fy mhen,
dwi'n geiban, ond yn gwybod
mai yma wyf inna i fod.

Where the boats of the poor
say their piece to the waves,
and there are two hours between me and the day,
two hours in filthy weather,
it's a mess, and there's no star
above for me tonight,
I'm wrecked but I recognise
that I've washed up where I should be.

(translations by Grahame Davies)

GERWYN WILIAMS

Molawd Pry Genwair

Pwy wêl fai arno,
yn cilio'n reddfol rhag gilotîn fy rhaw
ac ymdoddi i'r ddaear drachefn?
Hawdd deall ei sgeptigiaeth,
y sbageti tryloyw
sy'n arnofio'n ddigoesau
i lawr lôn goch y pridd.
Mor gomig ei amddiffyniad pan gaiff ei ddaearu:
ymbelennu fel draenog
— wedi colli ei bigau!

Gwron di-asgwrn-cefn,
nid yr un yw amodau ei arwriaeth....
Pa ryfedd ei fod am herio
tynged sinicaidd ei enw —
cael ei nyddu ar fachyn
i dynnu cymrodyr o'u cynefin,
o dangnefedd y dŵr i olau dydd eu tranc?
Onid hwn yw halen y ddaear,
hwsmon yr encilion
sy'n hidlo'r tir a'i baratoi?

Mabolgampwr lastig,
diarhebol ei benderfyniad,
yn dal ati'n ffyddiog yn y tywyllwch islaw
yn nannedd y diolchgarwch angheuol uwchlaw.

In Praise of an Earthworm

Who can blame him,
as he shrinks instinctively from the spade's guillotine
and fuses again with earth?
Easy to grasp his scepticism,
transparent spaghetti
that slips without legs
down the red lane of the soil.
Such a comical defence when he's unearthed:
to ball himself up like a hedgehog
who's lost his prickles.

Spineless hero,
for him heroism's terms are not the same....
No wonder he challenges
the cynical destiny of his name —
twisted on a hook
to tempt fellow-creatures from their haunts,
from the serenity of water to death by daylight.
Is he not the salt of the earth,
a bailiff of nooks and crannies
who filters soil and conditions it?

Elastic athlete,
unrivalled for resolution,
still burrowing away in the darkness below,
outbraving the lethal gratitude up above.

Note: Pry genwair, the Welsh for earthworm,
literally means "fishing-rod fly".

Adduned

Oherwydd dy ddodi'n fy mreichiau,
yn amddifad 'rôl magwrfa'r groth;

oherwydd dy wythbwys mewn clorian,
tunnell o gyfrifoldeb mewn côl;

oherwydd i'th lygaid daflunio
brysnegeseuon cudd rhyngom ni;

oherwydd iti blethu dy ddwylaw
fel adyn yn erfyn maddeuant;

oherwydd hyn oll, Marged Elen,
seiren wyt ti sy'n fflachio'n fy mhen,

fy ambiwlans ar alwad barhaus,
boed derfysg, boed hindda, boed eira,

o fore gwyn tan gefn trymedd nos
yn aros, i'th ymgeleddu di.

Pledge

Because you're an infant in arms,
expelled from the nursery womb;

because you're eight pounds on the scales
and a ton of care in a cuddle;

because your eyes keep transmitting
cryptic telegrams between us;

because your plaited hands suggest
a wretch who's begging forgiveness;

because of all this, Marged Elen,
you're a siren flashing in my head,

I'm an ambulance always on call,
be it riot, fair weather or snow,

from sunrise to sultry midnight —
just waiting to succour you.

(translations by Richard Poole, with the author)

143

GRAHAME DAVIES

Coch

Ti'n gosod yr olewyddion gyda'r *feta*,
  a rhoi'r *ciabatta*'n barod at y cwrdd,
agor y coch, a dyro'r gwyn i oeri;
  a chynnau'r gannwyll bersawr ar y bwrdd.

Rhyw *antipasti* bach i godi archwaeth,
  a chwlffyn o *baguette* o Ffrainc gerllaw
rhyw beth fel hyn yw trafod achub Cymru
  yn CF Un ym mil naw nawdeg naw.

Tybed pa beth a wnâi o hyn, dy dadcu,
  a heriodd garchar er mwyn Yncl Joe,
yr un a gadwodd faner goch y chwyldro
  i chwifio drwy dridegau'r pentref glo?

Yr un a aeth i Rwsia ar wahoddiad
  i dderbyn Sofietaidd ddiolch-yn-fawr,
a dod yn ôl â cherflun bach o Lenin,
  sy'n addurn uwch dy silff-ben-tân di 'nawr.

Yr un enillodd lid y rhecsyn lleol
  am gyfarfodydd gweithwyr yn ei dŷ.
Tybed pa beth feddyliai ef o wyres,
  sy'n nashi dosbarth-canol bach fel ti?

Tybed yn wir. Ond merch dy dadcu wyt ti:
  dau o'r un brethyn mewn gwahanol ffyrdd,
yn ceisio cuddio creithiau anghyfiawnder
  drwy beintio'r byd i gyd yn goch — neu'n wyrdd.

Red

You set the olives down beside the *feta*,
    and make sure the *ciabatta's* looking nice.
You light the perfumed candle for the meeting,
    open the red wine, put the white on ice.

A little *antipasti* to begin with;
    a French *baguette* to soak up all that wine;
this is the way we meet to save our nation
    in CF One in nineteen ninety nine.

I wonder what he'd make of this, your grand-dad,
    who risked a prison cell for Stalin's sake,
the one who raised the red flag in the valleys,
    the man the hungry thirties couldn't break?

The one who got invited out to Russia
    to get the Soviets' thank-you face to face,
and came back with a little bust of Lenin,
    that's now an ornament above your fireplace.

The one who earned the local rag's displeasure
    for calling meetings to arouse the mass,
I wonder what he'd make of his descendant:
    Welsh-speaking, nationalistic, middle-class?

I wonder. But you're still so like your grand-dad:
    cut from the same cloth, just by different means,
trying to cure the evils of injustice
    by painting all the world in red — or green.

Villanelle y Cymoedd

'Rwy'n gweld mai teithio ydy pwrpas taith;
'rwy'n dechrau deall castiau ysbryd Duw,
a gweld mai ennill ffydd yw colli'r ffaith.

'Rwy'n gweld brawdgarwch dyddiol bro ddi-waith,
y hiwmor du a'r jocian yn y ciw,
'rwy'n gweld mai teithio ydy pwrpas taith.

Gweld plant y dôl yn gweithio dros yr iaith,
y Cymoedd yn pleidleisio "Ie" yn driw,
a gweld mai ennill ffydd yw colli'r ffaith.

Tro ar y mynydd wedi diwrnod gwaith;
y fam yn cario'i babi 'lan y rhiw,
'rwy'n gweld mai teithio ydy pwrpas taith.

'Rwy'n dechrau deall gras sy'n diodde'r graith,
a deall fel mae marw er mwyn byw;
a gweld mai ennill ffydd yw colli'r ffaith.

'Rwy'n teimlo'r gwynfyd yn y gwacter maith
a bendith llosg yr halen ar y briw.
'Rwy'n gweld mai teithio ydy pwrpas taith,
a gweld mai ennill ffydd yw colli'r ffaith.

Valley Villanelle

I see that it's to journey that we go;
I'm starting to discern the spirit's way,
I see it's only faith if you don't know.

The daily comradeship of men brought low,
the dole-queue jokes while waiting for your pay,
I see that it's to journey that we go.

The jobless kids who help the language grow,
the Valleys voting 'Yes' to have their say,
I see it's only faith if you don't know.

A walk up to the mountain for a blow:
the mother takes the baby out to play;
I see that it's to journey that we go.

I see, through grief, the grace that lies below,
and how, to live, you give your life away;
I see it's only faith if you don't know.

The burning blessing when the answer's no;
the stinging balm of silence when I pray.
I see that it's to journey that we go.
I see it's only faith if you don't know.

147

Rough Guide

Mae'n digwydd yn anorfod,
fel dŵr yn dod o hyd i'w lefel,
ond bob tro yr agoraf lawlyfr teithio
'rwy'n hwylio heibio'r prifddinasoedd
a'r golygfeydd,
ac yn tyrchu i strydoedd cefn diolwg
y mynegai,
a chael fy mod
yn Ffrainc, yn Llydawr;
yn Seland Newydd, Maori;
yn yr Unol Daleithiau — yn dibynnu ar ba ran —
'rwy'n Navajo, yn Cajun, neu'n ddu.

Y fi yw'r Cymro Crwydr;
yn Iddew ymhob man.
Heblaw, wrth gwrs, am Israel.
Yno, 'rwy'n Balesteiniad.

Mae'n rhyw fath o gymhlethdod, mae'n rhaid,
fy mod yn codi'r grachen ar fy psyche fel hyn.
Mi dybiaf weithiau sut beth a fyddai
i fynd i un o'r llefydd hyn
a jyst mwynhau.

Ond na, wrth grwydro cyfandiroedd y llyfrau teithio,
yr un yw'r cwestiwn ym mhorthladd pob pennod:
"Dinas neis. 'Nawr ble mae'r geto?"

Rough Guide

It happens inevitably,
like water finding its level:
every time I open a travel book,
I sail past the capital cities, the sights,
and dive straight into the backstreets of the index
to find that in France, I'm Breton;
in New Zealand, Maori;
in the U.S.A. — depending on which part —
I'm Navajo, Cajun, or black.

I'm the Wandering Welshman.
I'm Jewish everywhere.
Except, of course, in Israel.
There, I'm Palestinian.

It's some kind of a complex, I know,
that makes me pick this scab on my psyche.
I wonder sometimes what it would be like
to go to these places
and just enjoy.

No, as I wander the continents of the guidebooks,
whatever chapter may be my destination,
the question's always the same when I arrive:
"Nice city. Now where's the ghetto?"

(translations by the author)

HUW MEIRION EDWARDS

Hwiangerdd

Si hei lwli, ni a'r nos
Sy rhagor, a'r sêr agos,
A dim o'n blaenau ni'n dau
Ond atyniad y tonnau.

Ni a'r sêr, a'r dyfnder du
Odanom yn ein denu,
Suo-gân ei drwmgwsg o
Yn un alargan heno.

Ni a'r sêr bradwrus, oer,
A nos y treisio iasoer
Yn dy waed ac yn dy wedd,
Yn ddoe heb iddo ddiwedd.

Ddoe'n y cof am heddiw'n cau,
A chroth yn cuddio'i chreithiau.
Hon, y groth sydd heno'n grud,
Fydd hafan dy fedd hefyd.

Yn dy holl eiddilwch di,
Yn ddamwain, maddau imi.
Maddau im y camwedd hwn
Yn enw'r cnawd a rannwn.

Si hei lwli 'mabi, mae'n
Rhy oer, rhy hwyr i eiriau.
Heno'n neb yr hunwn ni
A'r don yn feddrod inni.

Lullaby

Si hei lwli, us and night
It is now, and the starlight,
And nothing now lies before
But the waves drawn to the shore.

Us and the stars, and the dark sea-deep
Beneath us invites us to sleep;
The lullaby of slumbering might
Is one long elegy tonight.

Now, with the icy stars above,
The night that rape murdered love
Taints your blood, marks your face
With treachery time won't erase.

We're prisoners of yesterday
And a womb that hides its scars away.
The cradle of your mother's womb
Tonight will be your haven-tomb.

In all your fragility,
Child of chance, pardon me.
Forgive this act of despair
In the name of the flesh we share.

Si hei lwli, sleep, my baby,
Too cold, too late for words from me.
Tonight, we nobodies, on the wave
We'll sleep. It shall be our grave.

(translation by Grahame Davies)

Glaw

(Medi 18-19, 1997)

A phob awr yn awr yn oes
a'n croesau'n inc oer eisoes,
daeth y smwclaw distaw, du
fel asid i'n diflasu.

Hen law blin drwy'r brifddinas
a'i choedlannau'n byllau bas,
glaw oer, mân yn treiglo i'r mêr
i wawdio'n tipyn hyder.

Yna gweld drwy'n gwydrau gwin
y wyrth rhwng crio a chwerthin,
y nos 'di cilio'n ddistaw,
a'n gwlith yn gymysg â'r glaw.

Rain

(September 18-19, 1997)

Now, our inky crosses dry
— each hour, eternity —
the silent, dismal drizzle
consumes us, chills us all.

Our city: rain sweeps through it
puddling on parkland and streets,
merciless, endless, mocking —
a rain to soak to the skin.

Glasses raised: our wish, our win!
torn between tears and laughing,
silently day is dawning
mingling our dew with the rain.

(translation by Elin ap Hywel)

ELIN LLWYD MORGAN

Sgitso Picasso

Eistedd ar y foryd
yn edrych ar y machlud
yn rhegi ffawd
a'r uwd o fyd
    codog
sy'n codi cyfog.

Dywedodd Picasso fod pob dynes
naill ai'n dduwies neu'n slebog.
Duwieslebog ydw i,
yn derbyn pobl ddrwg a da
i mewn i 'mywyd
yn llenwi bysys efo pobl neis
a syrthio mewn cariad efo'r misffits.

Mae'r machlud mor rhamantus
wrth iddo dreiddio
i dwll din yr ynys,
ond dwi ar goll er gwaetha'r
rhyw a'r rhamant a'r drygs a'r gwin
sy'n cadw'r duwiau dicllon draw.

Mae rhywbeth ar goll
yn fy mywyd colledig,
rhyw bechod dwi heb ei brofi,
rhyw dduw dwi heb ei ddofi
a'i wneud yn rhan annatod
o gymhlethdod fy nghymeriad.

Cyn i'r machlud fy sugno
i grombil ynysig unigrwydd,
estyn dy law i mi eto:
mi fydda i'n dduwies
ac yn slebog i ti,
yn sgitso i Bicasso.

Schizo de Picasso

Sitting by the inlet
looking at the sunset
cursing fate
and the crazy
mixed-up world
that makes my heart retch.

Picasso said that every woman
is either a goddess or a slut.
I am a goddesslut,
welcoming good and bad folk
into my life
filling buses with those that are nice
and falling in love with the misfits.

The sunset is so romantic
as it penetrates
the island's arsehole,
but I feel lost in spite of the
sex and drugs and rock 'n roll
that keep the killjoy gods at bay.

Something is missing
in my prodigal life,
some sin I haven't proven,
some god I haven't woven
into the complex pattern
of my make-up.

Before the sunset sucks me into
the beached bowels of loneliness,
reach your hand out for me again:
I'll be a goddess
and a slut for you,
a schizo for Picasso.

Holiadur Ofer

Os yw Duw yn bod,
wna i ddim bod mor naïf
â gofyn iddo pam bod
cymaint o ddioddefaint
yn y byd, na pham bod
crefydd, rhyw ac arian
wrth wraidd pob pechod.
Wna i ddim gofyn iddo
ei farn am leianod
neu os yw'n ffansïo
y slebog wisg-garpiog
sy'n llusgo 'i chartref
mewn bagiau plastig,
cymaint â'r dduwies ryw
ar gloriau sgleinliw
y cylchgronau pornograffig.
Wna i ddim gofyn iddo
os yw efengylwyr
yn mynd ar ei nerfau
neu os yw'n fwy cartrefol
mewn capeli neu dafarndai.
Wna i ddim gofyn iddo
os yw'n seinio ar y dôl
bob wythnos yn swyddfa
DHS y nefoedd tra'n
ysgrifennu ei draethawd
ymchwil diddiwedd, na
gofyn pwy fydd yn marcio.
Mae hyn yn amherthnasol,
fel holi os oes lle neilltuol
i mi yn ei gynllun oesoesol,
neu os mai Fo neu'r Diafol
sydd wrth lyw ffawd dragwyddol
y greadwriaeth bendramwnwgl.
Os yw Duw yn bod,
wna i ddim gofyn iddo....

Futile Questionnaire

If God exists,
I won't be so naïve
as to ask him why
there is so much
suffering in the world,
nor why religion,
sex and money
are at the root of all evil.
I won't ask him
his opinion about nuns
or whether he fancies
the raggedy baglady
who drags her home
in plastic bags
as much as the sex siren
on the glossy covers
of the porno mags.
I won't ask him
if evangelists
get on his nerves
or whether he feels
more at ease
in chapels or pubs.
I won't ask him
if he signs on the dole
every week in heaven's
DHS office while
writing his neverending
thesis, nor will I ask him
who'll be marking.
This is immaterial,
like asking if there is
a starring role for me
in his eternal movie,
or whether it is He or Satan
directing the X-rated creation.
If God exists,
I won't ask him....

(translations by the author)

157

CERI WYN JONES

Dylanwad

*(Mae teulu 'nhad yn hanu o Flaenau Ffestiniog
yng nghysgod y Moelwyn.)*

Os ofnaf na fedraf i
hel achau yn ei lechi
dienaid, na gweld yno'r
acenion cŷn ers cyn co',
na rhoi'n awr enw na hynt,
na bedd, na wyneb iddynt;
o hyd, y mae'r cyn-dadau
ym mêr fy mêr, ac y mae
rheg a chwys eu creigiau chwâl
yn finiog ar fy ana'l,
a chywyddau'r llechweddi
yn faen ar faen ynof i.

Y Gymrâg

Fe fu'n arafu eriôd, a'i dyddie'n
diweddu'n ddiddarfod,
a, bob awr, ers bore'i bod,
bu ei weindio yn boendod.

158

Influence

*(My father's family hail from Blaenau Ffestiniog,
which is overlooked by the Moelwyn mountains.)*

In these screes, I cannot see
a sign of my ancestry,
or find, in this slump of slates
their chisel strokes, undated,
nor find their names, their faces,
their gravestones, — a single trace.
And yet, my father's fathers
are in my bones, and they are
the tumbled rocks. They swear and sing,
a catch in my own breathing.
The metres of this country
are stone on stone inside me.

(translation by Elin ap Hywel)

The Welsh Language

Always it has been slowing, and its days
forever are ending,
and each day since its morning
it's been a pain, the winding.

(translation by Grahame Davies)

NICI BEECH

Camau Cyntaf

A minnau'n friwiau o fri,
yn storws o dosturi,
fel rhyw ddawn, a ddaw'n ddi-wad,
yn amlach fe ddaw'r teimlad.

Fo'n Jiwdas a fi'n jadan,
dyn a'i nerth sy'n 'ngwneud i'n wan.
Pam 'mod i, yn gi sy'n gaeth,
yn udo am warchodaeth?

Ond eto fyth, dwyt ti fawr
o arth-foi, dim byd gwerthfawr.
Un yfwr, un o nifer,
un llyfr o fewn blwyddlyfr blêr.
Un o griw i wella'r graith,
un neis — mi wnest am noswaith.

Ond heddiw y mae'r briwiau
mewn lliw ac er mwyn lleihau
y brad, rhaid cyrraedd y brig,
fi'n onest, a fi'n unig.

Ar ben ein rhestr roedd llestri
neis, ond mae'n hanrhegion ni
bellach yn geriach i'w gwared.
Creiriau ŷnt o golli cred.
Ai hyn yw ein gwahanu?
Rhyw focs o wydrau a fu
unwaith yn ein cyfuno?
Nadu clwyf wrth newid clo
ein cyd-fyw; codi dau fys
ar yr allor, ewyllys
rhannu ar chwâl, anialwch
sy'n y gegin, a'r llestri'n llwch.

First Steps

Plastered with bruises, a full tank of pity; undeniable as
instinct, the feeling sweeps over me:

He's a Judas; I'm a slut; his strength is sucking mine away.
Why am I, a chained dog, howling for my master?

And yet — you're not so special. Just another lager lout, one
entry in a tattered diary — someone to lick my wounds a
little — nice enough for a night.

Today, the bruises are technicolour. To soften the betrayal I
must rise above this, be honest, be myself.

Pretty china was top of our list: now our gifts are jumble to be
junked, relics of a loss of faith. Is this how we end? Over a
boxful of glasses we once drank from together?

I weep my wounds while I change the locks, stick the Vs up
at our marriage, the longing to share's been shattered, the
kitchen's a mess, the dishes all dust.

I close the curtains on yesterday, the huge great Yesterday
which weighed so heavy on my mind. Somehow it came and
went. This year is a very different challenge.

With my dream-catching net, I walk the path of confidence,
my faith in myself is my prop, my vow a white carpet before
me.

Do you see the boat setting off, anger steering her course?

This year is a clean slate.

Ar llynedd, 'rwy'n cau'r llenni,
Ar y Ddoe mawr oedd i mi
Yn fwrn, ond eto, fe aeth.
Ac eleni, rhagluniaeth
hollol wahanol yw'r her.

Troediaf ar hyd tir hyder
Gyda rhwyd hel breuddwydion
A hunan-ffydd i mi'n ffon,
F'adduned yn garped gwyn.

Welwch chi'r cwch yn cychwyn?
A llid yn ei llywio hi?

Llechan lân fydd eleni.

Dal Breuddwyd yn y Bore

Nid âf o wres y *duvet*
i benyd y byd. I be?
Mor llwm yw'r dydd a mor llwyd;
ni roddaf i fy mreuddwyd
unrhyw siawns iddi ddawnsio
i ffwrdd, ond mae hi ar ffo
eisoes; clywaf hi'n sisial
yn y dwr; ceisiaf ei dal
yn fy mhen cyn i lenni'r
dydd fynd â dy wyneb di.

Holding a Dream

I won't leave the warm duvet
to suffer the world. No way.
For such a grey, bleak daybreak
I will not, for any's sake
let my dream just dance away —
but still, it's going its own way;
like water; I can't stop the flow
but I must catch it somehow
before the light displaces
all vestiges of your face.

(translations by Elin ap Hywel)

MERERID PUW DAVIES

Dros *Apéritif*

Tyrd fy lleu
heno
mi gawn fod yn greulon

a denu honno a elwir "Cariad"
o dras difeddwl y tylwyth teg

na challia fyth
na chofia fyth
adael ei gwyrdd adenydd brau bregus
gartref
pan ehed fel haf heibio

cawn fod yn greulon
a galw hon

yr annwyl blentyn
ei gwên yn ddiniwed
gerddi'n ei gwallt
dail disglair yn rhodd yn ei dwylo

cawn alw hon
a elwir "Cariad"

ac mewn dial am rywbeth
nas cofiwn yn iawn
cawn eillio ei gwallt
trywanu ei dwylo
llosgi ei llygaid

a rhyngom dan wenu
racsio a rhwygo
dros *apéritif*

yr adenydd gwyrdd gwirion gloyw.

Over an *Apéritif*

Come, light of my life,
tonight
let's be cruel

let's seduce the little girl they call 'Love',
that thoughtless nymph —

who never wises up,
never remembers
to leave her frail green wings
at home
when she flies by, like summer

let's be cruel
and call her

our darling child
with her innocent smile
her hair full of flowers
her hands clasped full of bright leaves

let's call the one
they call 'Love'

and in revenge
for something half forgotten
let's shave her hair
stab her hands
burn her eyes

and between us, smiling,
over an *apéritif*
let's slash and tear

the fragile, shining green wings.

Mae'r Cyfrifiadur Hefyd Yn Fardd

Caewn y drws. Boddwn bob sŵn. Mae hon yn ddefod. Agorwn
gaead pistyll y trydan.

Sgwrsiwn.

Dyma ymddiddan trwy wydr. Dyma ymgom mewn geiriau
bach neon
byw, pryfed tân yng ngardd ffurfiol y sgrîn, heb ddim o gyffwrdd
amrwd ansicr yr un llaw ar ddarfodedig dudalen.

Sgwrsiwn.

Nid yw'r cyfrifiadur yma'n fawr gwahanol i'r rheini all
reoli calonnau a gweithio gwyddorau bywyd.

Ac nid yw'r cyfrifiadur, yn ei wefrau a'i olau, fawr ddim
yn wahanol

i wefrau a golau fy nghalon i.

Sgwrsiwn.

Rydym mewn gwlad dramor. Dysgaf fy iaith iddo.

A daw atebion pefr, fel petai o du arall Ewrop, yn
gwifreiddio yn wefr a golau i gyd. Dim ond y cyfrifiadur a fi
sy'n deall.

Sgwrsiwn.

A'm hiaith fy hun, fy nhestun cyfarwydd: fe'u gwelaf yn
newid eu gwedd —

yn arwyneb arian, yn flodeuged amryliw, yn orymdaith
syfrdanol, yn llateion llachar, yn ddisgleiriach na dim a welwyd
erioed.

Sgwrsiwn. Mae'r cyfrifiadur yn fardd.

The Computer is a Poet too

Let us close the door, shut out all noise. This is a ritual. Let us un-
cover the source of the current.

Let us talk.

This is conversation through glass. A discourse in small, quick
neon words,
fireflies in the formal garden of the screen, nothing to do with
the gauche, tentative touch of one hand on a forgotten page.

Let us talk.

This computer is not much different to the ones which control
hearts and run the processes of life.

And the computer, with its pulses and light, is not much different
to the pulses and light in my heart.

Let us talk.

We are in a foreign country. I teach it my language.

And shining replies come to me, as if from a distant country, their
pulses and light thrill me. Only the computer and I
understand them.

Let us talk.

And my own language, my familiar text: I see them changing their
form — into a silver surface, a multicoloured bouquet, an amazing
procession, shining messengers, brighter than anything
ever before seen.

We talk. The computer is a poet.

(translations by Elin ap Hywel)

ELINOR WYN REYNOLDS

Y Gynddaredd

(i J.G.)

Cafodd ei gnoi, ei gyffroi
gan gi gwallgo',
a nawr, mae'n chwilio am gysur,
am gysgod, am waed.
Nid pawb sy'n gweld y bwystfil, nid pawb sy'n edrych i fyw
ei lygaid
i weld y golau gwahanol yn y canhwyllau cyson
a gweld y boen a'r angen ynddo am gynhesrwydd a pheth
maldod.
Mae'n rheibio plant pan nad yw neb yn edrych a'u gadael
yn sypiau o esgyrn
heb lef nac ymbil ar ôl ynddynt.
Cymer fantais o hen bobl nad oes ganddynt neb i'w hamddiffyn
ac wedi iddyn' nhw ffwndro a malu awyr am anghenfil
yn darnio'u dillad a llyfu'u cyrff er mwyn sugno'r mêr o'u
hesgyrn,
'does yna neb yn eu credu.
Anadla'n gynnes ar war ambell fenyw sy'n ddigon ffôl i
gerdded adref
wrth ei hun yn y tywyllwch
sy'n ddigon i wneud iddi redeg adref
a'i henaid yn llumanu y tu ôl iddi,
ei chalon yn ei dwylo'n fregus.
Bratha'r gŵr sydd am ei ddifa;
suddo'i ddannedd yn ddwfn i'w gnawd
gan rwygo'r cig oddi ar gadwyn gwythïen frau,
y fath drydan, y fath wefr.
Ond mae'r newyn yn dal i fod yno
a'r angen yn fwy a mwy.

Rabid

(for J.G.)

He was bitten, damaged
by a mad dog,
and now, he is looking for comfort,
for shelter, for blood.
Not everybody sees the beast, not everybody looks deep into
                                       his eyes
to see the different light in those constant candles,
to see the pain and the need in him for warmth and some
                                      tenderness.
He ravages children when nobody is looking, leaving them
                                   as piles of bone
without voice or plea left in them.
He takes advantage of old people who have nobody to
                                   defend them
and after they have lost their minds and talked nonsense
                                 about a monster
that ripped their clothes and licked their bodies to suck out
                            the marrow from their bones
nobody believes them.
He breathes warm breaths on the necks of those women
                       who are foolish enough to walk home
alone in the dark;
it is enough to make them run home,
souls streaming out behind them,
hearts fragile in their hands.
He bites the man who wants to destroy him;
sinks his teeth deep into his flesh
ripping the meat from the delicate chain of veins,
such electricity, such thrills.
But he still has his hunger
and the need gets bigger.

Mae 'na ddynion yn gorwedd mewn caeau
ym mhob man drwy Gymru

Pan ddaw'n dymor gorweddian
a'r haul yn ei hwyliau'n hongain
yn beryglus o isel oddi ar ganghennau a bargodion,
mae'r dynion yn ymddangos yn y glaswellt
mewn caeau ar ochr heolydd,
dan goed yn llonydd,
wrth fôn cloddiau ac ar lan afonydd,
ger hen byllau glo a mewn mynwentydd
yn eistedd, yn ystyried, yn pwyso a mesur, yn cnoi cil,
yn gwylio, yn macsu meddyliau, yn corddi breuddwydion.
Daeth yr haf ag amser newydd gyda hi
yn gwmwl gwybed digon diog i ddrysu
bysedd cloc.
Ac o'r lleiniau lle mae amser yn llonydd
mae'r dynion mudan yn gorffwys ar eu breichiau
ac edrych ar fwrlwma trwstlyd
y gweddill chwyslyd
yn glymau o geir a negeseuon.
Bob yn un, symuda eu llygaid tuag at y gorwel tawel
sy'n gyson wastad
ac o'r fan honno, pwyso yn ôl i gôl y gwair
a syllu i fyw llygad yr haul.

There are men lying in fields throughout Wales

When the season for lazing comes
and the sun hangs in ecstasy,
dangerously low from branches and eaves,
the men appear in the grass,
in fields at roadsides,
under trees like statues,
in hedgerows and on river banks,
by old coal mines and in cemeteries
they sit, consider, mull, chew over,
watch, brew thoughts, twist dreams.
The summer brought a new time with her
in clouds of flies so lazy they confuse
the hands on clock faces.
And from the glades where time stands still
the quiet men rest on their arms
and look at the noisy movement
of the others sweating in
a knot of cars and errands.
One by one their eyes move towards the silent horizon
that is constant always
from there, they lean back into the grass's grip
and stare the sun straight in the eye.

(translations by the author)

Acknowledgements/Cydnabyddiaethau

Oliver Reynolds

"Reading" is from *Skevington's Daughter* (Faber 1985); "The Player Queen's Wife" is from *The Player Queen's Wife* (Faber , 1987); "The Gap", "Greek", and "The Almost" are from *Almost*, (Faber, 1999). "Evening", a verson of Rilke's "Abend", originally appeared in the *TLS*.

Catherine Fisher

"In a Chained Library", "I. 13th April 1769, Matavai, Oteheite" (The Unexplored Ocean) are from *The Unexplored Ocean* (Seren, 1994); "Cimabue's Crucifix", "Undertakers", "Fimbulwinter", and "Vampire Ballet" all appear in *Altered States* (Seren, 1999).

Don Rodgers

"Moontan", "The Suffering of Fishes", "Wolf-whistling for One" are from *Moontan* (Seren, 1996); "Mariposa", "The Big Battalions", "Burry Holm", and "Tycoch" appear in *Multiverse* (Seren, 2000).

Paul Henry

"For X and Y" is from *Captive Audience* (Seren, 1996), "The Last Throws of Summer", "Lines Written Outside a "'Replica of a Sunshine Home for Blind Babies', Aberystwyth", "Welsh Incident", and "Newport East" are all from *The Milk Thief* (Seren, 1998); "The Slipped Leash" appeared in the *Times Literary Supplement*. "Slipping on Leaves" appeared in *Planet*. "Boys" is published here for the first time.

Gwyneth Lewis

"Pentecost", "The Hedge", "V (Welsh Espionage*)*", and "Advice on Adultery" are from *Parables and Faxes* (Bloodaxe, 1995). "I. Prologue, III, V, VI, VII" are from the title poem in *Zero Gravity* (Bloodaxe, 1998).

Stephen Knight

"The Big Parade", "After Lessons", "The Desert Inn", "Elvis", and "The Mermaid Tank" all appear in *Dream City Cinema* (Bloodaxe, 1996). "So Early in the Year" was first publised in *London Review of Books*.

Anna Wigley
"The Last Cobbler in Canton" has appeared in *Staple*, "Duck Shooting" featured in the 1999 *Exeter Anthology*, "Big Weekend"and "Boxing Day to Lidney" appear here for the first time.

Samantha Wynne Rhydderch
"The X-Ray Room", "The Phonebook Errata" and "The Bridesmaids' Reply" have all appeared in *Poetry Wales*. "The Lighthouse Keeper's Daughter" and "Pope Gregory XI's Bedroom" have been published in a pamphlet, *Stranded on Ithaca* (Redbeck Press, 1998). "The Breakdown" and "Lighting the Fire" appear here for the first time.

Zoë Skoulding
"Trappist Brewers", "Eclipse", and "Gibraltar" have appeared in *Poetry Wales*; "Sledging", "Kraftwerk", and "Map" were published in her book, *Tide Table* (Gwasg Pantycelyn, 1998).

Deryn Rees-Jones
"The Memory Tray" is the title poem from *The Memory Tray* (Seren, 1994). "My Father's Hair", "The One That Got Away", "What It's Like To Be Alive", "Calcium" and "Snow Song" were published in *Signs Round a Dead Body* (Seren, 1998).

Frances Williams
"Descent", "Test Ahead", "The Tall Man", "What Survives", "Oyster Eating", "Bed Time", and "The Actress" are all from *Wild Blue* (Seren, 2000).

Fiona Sampson
"Green Thought" won the Newdigate Prize and was first published in *Picasso's Men* (Phoenix Press, 1994); "Pastoral from a Millennial Pattern Book" first appeared in *Alternatives: Social Transformation and Humane Governance*; "Legal and Tender" and "About the House" were first published in *Interchange*. "The Misunderstanding" and "The X File" appeared in *Agenda*.

Sarah Corbett
"Dream of a Horse", "My Mother's Lover", "The Red Wardrobe", and "Letter to a Lover" are from *The Red Wardrobe* (Seren, 1998). "My Son The Horse", "Harvest", and "Tooth Magic" appear here for the first time.

Kate Bingham
"Oxygen", "Things I learned at University", "Two friends meet for lunch...", "Face to Face", "In Passing", "Beaujolais", and "How to Play" are from *Cohabitation* (Seren, 1998). "6th December 1998" appears here for the first time.

Owen Sheers
"Hedge Foal", "Harvest", "Learning the Language", "Stammerer on Scree", "Night Bus", "Sea Reading", and "Stopped in the Street" are from *The Blue Book* (Seren, 2000).

Karen Goodwin
"Wolf", "The Summerhouse", "Brynhildr", and "The Sin-Eaters" have appeared in *Poetry Wales*. "Ancient", "Ballet", "Salome", and "Fallen Star" appear here for the first time.

Emyr Lewis
"Mewn Eglwys" is from *Chwarae Mig* (Barddas, 1995); "Rhyddid" won the National Eisteddfod Crown in 1998 and was published in *Cyfansoddiadau a Beirniadaethau Eisteddfod Genedlaethol Bro Ogwr 1998* (Eisteddfod Genedlaethol Cymru, 1998).

Iwan Llwyd
"Iawn, gei di ofyn cwestiwn personol" and "Dan Ddylanwad" are from *Dan Ddylanwad* (Gwasg Taf, 1997).

Gwyneth Lewis
"Rhodd" is from *Cyfrif Un ac Un yn Dri* (Barddas, 1996); "Adroddiad y Patholegydd" appears in *Y Llofrudd Iaith* (Barddas, 1999).

Ifor ap Glyn
"Tri Darlleniad Trychinebus Ynys Prydain 1" is from *Golchi Llestri Mewn Bar Mitzvah* (Gwasg Carreg Gwalch, 1998); selections from "Y Golau yn y Gwyll" which won the National Eisteddfod Crown in 1999, are taken from *Cyfansoddiadau a Beirniadaethau Eisteddfod Genedlaethol Ynys Môn 1999* (Eisteddfod Genedlaethol Cymru, 1999).

Twm Morys
"Sefyll 'Rown" and "Y Teithiwr" are from *Ofn Fy Het* (Barddas, 1995); "Mi Gan Nhw Ddisgwyl" appears here for the first time.

Elin ap Hywel
"Deall Goleuni" is from *Tu Chwith 6*, Autumn 1996; "Duwiesau" is from *Poetry Wales* 34.2, Oct. 1998; "Cawl" and "Defnyddiol" appear here for the first time.

Meirion MacIntyre Huws
"Côt" is from *Talwrn y Beirdd 9* (Gwasg Gwynedd, 1998); "Lle mae cychod y tlodion" appeared in *Cywyddau Cyhoeddus 3* (Gwasg Carreg Gwalch, 1998).

Gerwyn Wiliams
"Molawd Pry Genwair" and "Adduned" are from *Cydio'n Dynn* (Y Lolfa, 1997).

Grahame Davies
"Coch" is from *Barddas 255*, Nov/Dec 1999; "Villanelle y Cymoedd" and "Rough Guide" appear here for the first time.

Huw Meirion Edwards
"Hwiangerdd" is from *Barddas 245*, Mar/Apr 1998; "Glaw" is from *Cywyddau Cyhoeddus 3*, (Gwasg Carreg Gwalch, 1998).

Elin Llwyd Morgan
"Sgitso Picasso" and "Holiadur Ofer" are from *Duwieslebog* (Y Lolfa, 1993).

Ceri Wyn Jones
"Y Gymrâg" is from *Taliesin 107*, Autumn 1999; "Dylanwad" appears here for the first time.

Nici Beech
"Camau Cyntaf" is from *Taliesin 105/6*, Spring/Summer 1999; "Dal Breuddwyd yn y Bore" appears here for the first time.

Mererid Puw Davies
"Dros Apéritif" and "Mae'r cyfrifiadur Hefyd Yn Fardd" are from *Caneuon o Ben Draw'r Byd* (Y Lolfa, 1996).

Elinor Wyn Reynolds
"Y Gynddaredd" and "Mae 'na ddynion yn gorwedd..." are from *Poetry Wales* 33.2, Oct 1997.

The Poets/Y Beirdd

Oliver Reynolds (b. 1957) was born in Cardiff and educated at Hull University. He is the author of four collections of verse: *Skevington's Daughter* (1985), *The Player Queen's Wife* (1987), *The Oslo Tram* (1991) and *Almost* (1999), all published by Faber. He lives in London.

Catherine Fisher (b. 1957) was born in Wales where she still lives. She is a prize-winning author of children's novels, including *The Conjurer's Game*, shortlisted for the Smarties Prize. An accomplished poet, she has won the Cardiff International Poetry Competition and was awarded an Arts Council of Wales Prize for her first collection *Immrama* (Seren, 1988). *The Unexplored Ocean* appeared in 1995 and *Altered States* in 1999 (both Seren). A teacher for ten years, she now works as a freelance author, broadcaster and adjudicator.

Don Rodgers (b. 1957) was born in London and educated at Oxford. He has had poems published in a variety of magazines, newspapers and anthologies. His plays and short stories have been published, performed, and broadcast on BBC Radio 4, and he is a former winner of both the Drama Association of Wales Playwriting Competition and the One Voice Monologue Competition. His recent collection of poems is *Multiverse* (Seren, 2000). He works in Swansea, and lives near Neath.

Paul Henry (b. 1959) combines freelance writing and tutoring with part-time work as a Careers Adviser. Born in Aberystwyth and originally a singer-songwriter, he received an Eric Gregory Award for a draft of his first collection, *Time Pieces* (Seren, 1991). Two further books — *Captive Audience* (Seren, 1996) and *The Milk Thief* (Seren, 1998) — have since appeared and his poetry has been widely anthologised. He has edited *Poetry Wales* and was recently awarded an Arts Council of Wales Writer's Bursary.

Gwyneth Lewis (b. 1959) was born in Cardiff and studied English at Cambridge, Creative Writing at Columbia University, USA and wrote a doctorate on Iolo Morganwg at Oxford. She has published five collections of poetry, three in Welsh and two in English. *Parables and Faxes* (Bloodaxe, 1995 was short-listed for the Forward Prize and won the Aldeburgh Poetry Festival Prize. *Zero Gravity*

(Bloodaxe, 1998) was a PBS Recommendation. *Sonedau Redsa* was published by Gomer in 1990. *Cyfrif Un ac Un yn Dri* (Barddas) appeared in 1996 and *Y Llofrudd Iaith* (Barddas) in 1999. Her last four books were shortlisted for Welsh Book of the Year. She lives in Cardiff and works in television.

Stephen Knight (b. 1960) was born in Swansea and read English at Oxford. He is the author of several collections of poetry: *Flowering Limbs* (1993) and *Dream City Cinema* (1996), both published by Bloodaxe, and *The Sandfields Baudelaire* (Smith/Doorstop, 1996). His first novel, *Mr Schnitzel*, appeared from Penguin in 2000. He received an Eric Gregory Award in 1987 and won the 1992 National Poetry Competition.

Anna Wigley (b. 1962) has lived in Cardiff all her life. She has completed a PhD in English at Cardiff University. Her poetry has appeared in numerous magazines. She now works as a freelance writer and book reviewer.

Samantha Wynne Rhydderch (b. 1966) comes from a seafaring family in Newquay, West Wales. She studied Classics at Cambridge and Creative Writing at Cardiff University. In 1996 she received an award from the Arts Council of Wales to write her first pamphlet, *Stranded on Ithaca* (Redbeck Press, 1998). Her new book *Rockclimbing in Silk* is due from Seren in 2001.

Zoë Skoulding (b. 1967) grew up on the Norfolk-Suffolk border and lived in India before arriving in North Wales in 1991. She teaches in a secondary school and is editor of *Skald* poetry magazine, which she launched in 1994. With her husband, Alan Holmes, she has been involved in various musical projects. Her first collection of poetry, *Tide Table* (Gwasg Pantycelyn), appeared in 1998.

Deryn Rees-Jones (b. 1968) was born in Liverpool, studied in Bangor and London and is now Reader in Poetry at Liverpool Hope University College where she co-ordinates the MA in Creative Arts: Writing and Reading Poetry. Her most recent collection is *Signs Round a Dead Body* (Seren, 1998). Widely published, she has edited *Poetry Wales* and is also the author of critical works.

Frances Williams (b. 1968) was born in Bridgend. Her first volume of poetry, *Flotsam*, was published when she was just nineteen. She went on to study sculpture at Chelsea College of Art before becoming an editor and journalist, founding *Diva* magazine and then freelancing for *Time Out* and various national newspapers. In 1998 she won an Eric Gregory Award from the Society of Authors. Her second collection, *Wild Blue* (Seren) , appeared in 2000.

Fiona Sampson (b. 1968) is from Aberystwyth. Her publications are *Picasso's Men* (Phoenix Press, 1994); *The Self on the Page* (Jessica Kingsley, 1997); *The Healing Word* (The Poetry Society, 1999) and, forthcoming, an edition of co-translations with Jaan Kaplinski. Her collection of poetry will appear from Seren in 2001. She has received awards from the Society of Authors, Oppenheimer-John Downes, the Arts Council of Wales, the Millay Colony New York and the Newdigate Prize. She is Director of the Stephen Spender Memorial Trust.

Sarah Corbett (b. 1970) grew up in north Wales. After graduating she lived in eastern Europe and taught English. In 1997 she recieved an Eric Gregory Award and her first collection, *The Red Wardrobe* (Seren, 1998) was shortlisted for a Forward Prize and the T.S. Eliot Prize. She completed an MA in Creative Writing from the University of East Anglia in 1998 and now lives and writes in various parts of the UK with her husband and baby son.

Kate Bingham (b. 1971). Since leaving Oxford, Kate Bingham has worked in publishing and television. As well as her poetry collection, *Cohabitation* (Seren, 1998), she has written two novels, *Mummy's Legs* (1998) and *Slipstream* (2000), both published by Virago, and a screenplay for the BBC. She received an Eric Gregory Award for her poetry in 1996. She lives in London with her husband and daughter.

Owen Sheers (b. 1974) was born in Suva, Fiji and brought up in Abergavenny. Educated at Oxford and the Creative Writing programme at the University of East Anglia, he is the recipient of a 1999 Eric Gregory Award and the 1999 Vogue Young Writers award. His first collection is *The Blue Book* (Seren, 2000). He lives in London where he works in television production.

Karen Goodwin (b. 1976) was born in Swansea and studied English at Aberystwyth University. Having recently completed a masters degree in Creative Writing at the University of East Anglia, she is currently working on her first collection of poems. Her work has appeared in a number of magazines and anthologies and she received an Eric Gregory Award from the Society of Authors in 2000.

Emyr Lewis (b. 1957) was born in London and brought up in Cardiff. He was educated at Cambridge University, where he read English, and the University College of Wales, Aberystwyth. He is a master of *cynghanedd*, and has won many prizes, including both the Chair and Crown at the National Eisteddfod. His collection, *Chwarae Mig*, (Barddas) appeared in 1995.

Iwan Llwyd (b. 1957) was born in Llanidloes and brought up in Tal-y-bont, Conwy and Bangor. He was educated at the University College of Wales, Aberystwyth. His most recent collection of poems is *Dan Ddylanwad* (Gwasg Taf, 1997). He is also the author of *Sonedau Bore Sadwrn* (Y Lolfa, 1981), *Dan Anesthetig* (Gwasg Taf, 1987) and *Dan Fy Ngwynt* (Gwasg Taf, 1992). He won the Crown at the National Eisteddfod in 1990. Widely published, he has also collaborated on television scripts featuring poetry with Michael Bayley Hughes.

Ifor ap Glyn (b. 1961) is a London Welshman who has now settled in Caernarfon. Author of two volumes, *Holl Garthion Pen Cymro Ynghyd* (Y Lolfa, 1991) and *Golchi Llestri Mewn Bar Mitzvah* (Gwasg Carreg Gwalch, 1998), he performs his work regularly, both with and without musical accompaniment, and claims to be the only Welsh language poet to have been played on Radio 1 and to have performed alongside Tom Jones! He is currently touring a multi-media version of *Golau yn y Gwyll* with accompanying video and simultaneous English translation.

Twm Morys (b. 1961) was born in Oxford and brought up at Llanystumdwy and in Cwm Grwyne Fechan. He was educated at the University College of Wales, Aberystwyth and worked as a researcher for the BBC and as a lecturer before becoming a freelance writer and singer. His collection of poems, *Ofn Fy Het* (Barddas), appeared in 1995. It includes poems in strict metres as well as songs that he has recorded with his group, *Bob Delyn a'r Ebillion*. He is the son of Jan Morris and has collaborated with her on several books, including *Wales, the First Place* (1982). He lives in Llanystumdwy and Brittany.

Elin ap Hywel (b. 1962) (see Translator's Notes)

Meirion MacIntyre Huws (b 1963) was born and raised in Caernarfon and now lives in nearby Llanwnda. He graduated in Civil and Structural Engineering from the University of Wales, Cardiff and then worked for Dŵr Cymru for 16 years before becoming a graphic designer in 1996. He won the Chair at the National Eisteddfod in 1993 and is a regular participant in poetry contests. His first volume, *Y Llong Wen*, appeared in 1996. He is married with two sons.

Gerwyn Wiliams (b. 1963) is a native of Caernarfonshire. He graduated in Welsh from UCW Aberystwyth, where he was later awarded a PhD. In 1994 he won the Crown in the National Eisteddfod for a series of poems entitled 'Dolenni'. In 1997 his study of Welsh prose regarding the First World War, *Tir Neb,* was named Arts Council of Wales Welsh Language Book of the Year. His most recent collection of poems is *Cydio'n Dynn* (Y Lolfa, 1997). An ex-editor of the Welsh literary journal, *Taliesin*, he is currently Senior Lecturer in Welsh at the University of Wales, Bangor.

Grahame Davies (b. 1964)(see *The Editors* section)

Huw Meirion Edwards (b. 1965) was brought up in Llanfairpwll and Cardiff. He has a degree in French and Welsh from the University of Wales, Bangor, and has done research in medieval poetry at Jesus College, Oxford. He has been a lecturer at the Department of Welsh at the University of Wales, Aberystwyth, since 1992.

Elin Llwyd Morgan (b. 1966) was born in Cefnbrynbrain, Carmarthenshire. After graduating in French and Spanish at the University of Wales, Aberystwyth, she worked as a newspaper reporter and then as editor of Y Lolfa publishing company. She has published a guide to the pubs of Wales, *Tafarnau Cymru* (1992), and a volume of poems, *Duwieslebog* (Y Lolfa, 1993), and is a regular contributor of poems, reviews and articles to Welsh periodicals. She is now a freelance translator and writer, living in Dyffryn Ceiriog with her partner and son.

Ceri Wyn Jones (b. 1967) was born in Hertfordshire, but raised in Pembrokeshire and Ceredigion where he played international under 18 rugby until injury forced premature retirement. He graduated in English from UCW Aberystwyth before taking a teaching certificate at the same university. He has won the National Inter-Collegiate Chair in 1990, the Chair at the Urdd Eisteddfod in 1992 and the National Eisteddfod Chair in 1997 as well as being a member of winning bardic teams in the popular radio and tv series *Talwrn y Beirdd*. He is also Head of the English Department at Ysgol Dyffryn Teifi, Llandysul.

Nici Beech (b. 1969) was born in St. Asaph and grew up in Llangernyw, near Abergele. She was educated at Ysgol y Creuddyn, Bae Penrhyn, and graduated in Law from the University of Wales College, Cardiff, in 1992. After living and working in the Caernarfon area for over six years, she is now working at S4C Television in Cardiff as an Editorial Assistant in the Children's Department.

Mererid Puw Davies (b. 1970) was brought up in Lancashire and Clwyd. Later, she divided her time between Oxford and the continent, and carried out feminist research in German literature before taking up a post as a Lecturer in the German Department of UCL in London. She is a former winner of the Urdd Eisteddfod Literature Medal and Crown.

Elinor Wyn Reynolds (b. 1970) was born in Treorchy and brought up in Carmarthen. She read Welsh at Aberystwyth and Oxford Universities. Widely published in magazines and in various antholgies such as *O'r lawn Ryw*, *Dal Cêr*, and *Ffŵl Yn Y Dŵr*, she has worked at Tŷ Newydd Writers' Centre and Theatr Mwldan, Cardigan, and is resident poet on Roy Noble's radio programme on BBC Radio Wales. She currently works as a freelance writer, tutor and broadcaster and will be touring Wales in 2001 with a multimedia poetry show *Lliwiau Rhyddid* for Cwmni Theatr Bara Caws along with poet Ifor ap Glyn.

181

Note to the Translations/Nodyn Cyfieithwyr

Free verse poems are rendered in a similar English free verse form while formal poems not in *cynghanedd* are rendered into English rhyme and metre schemes very similar to the original with the exception of Twm Morys' "Sefyll 'Rown", "Y Teithiwr" and "Mi Gan Nhw Ddisgwyl", which are changed to free verse. As for poems in *cynghanedd*, a variety of translation approaches has been taken, although in no case is the internal alliteration of the *cynghanedd* replicated: "Hwiangerdd", "Glaw", "Y Gymrâg", "Dylanwad" and "Dal Breuddwyd yn y Bore" are all translated into stress, syllable and rhyme patterns approximating to those of the original poems. "Camau Cyntaf" and "Lle mae Cychod y Tlodion" are rendered into free verse, while "Côt" is put into a mock-heroic lyric form, which it was felt was a better English vehicle for a light-hearted poem than a replication of that poem's original metre would have been.

The Translators/Y Cyfieithwyr

Elin ap Hywel is a poet, translator and editor who works in Welsh and English. She was born in Colwyn Bay and brought up in various parts of Wales, including Wrexham and Aberystwyth. She graduated in Celtic Studies and spent time researching in Ireland. Her own work has been widely anthologised and translated into Czech, English, German, Italian and Japanese. Her publications include *Pethau Brau* (Y Lolfa, 1982) and she has edited two collections of Welsh women's short stories in English for Honno: *Luminous and Forlorn* (1994) and *Power* (1998). She now lives in Cardiff where she works as a translator for the National Museums and Galleries of Wales.

Richard Poole was born in Bradford and educated at Bradford Grammar School and UCNW Bangor. He teaches Creative Writing and English Literature at Coleg Harlech. His publications include four books of poems and a critical biography of Richard Hughes. He edited *Poetry Wales* magazine between 1992 and 1996. His translations of Gwyneth Lewis have appeared in publications in America, England and Wales.

The Editors/Y Golygwyr

Grahame Davies was born near Wrexham, studied English at Anglia University, Cambridge, and has a PhD in Welsh from Cardiff University. He is Welsh Language Editor of *Poetry Wales*. His books include *Adennill Tir* (Barddas, 1997) which won the Harri Webb Poetry Prize, and *Sefyll yn y Bwlch* (University of Wales Press, 1999), a volume of literary criticism. A BBC Wales journalist, he lives in Cardiff with his wife and two daughters.

Amy Wack was born in Florida, raised in California, educated at San Diego State University and completed a Masters degree in Creative Writing at Columbia University in New York. She is Reviews Editor for *Poetry Wales* magazine and has worked as the Poetry and Drama Editor at Seren for some years now. Her popular anthology of Seren poetry, *Burning the Bracken*, appeared in 1996. She lives with her husband and daughter in Cardiff.